The Amazing
Body Human

The Amazing Body Human

God's Design for Personhood

Mark P. Cosgrove

BAKER BOOK HOUSE
Grand Rapids, Michigan 49506

To

Jo Ann

Contents

Acknowledgments

I would like to express my sincere appreciation to the many people who helped me in the many stages of this book. My thanks goes to Dr. Richard Stanislaw and Taylor University, who allowed this psychologist to teach in areas not exclusively psychological. As with other writer-teachers my many thanks are also due to some very special students for their interest and helpful questions. Nancy Gore typed the final manuscript and made many helpful editorial suggestions. Dale Sloat and Jerry Hodson of Taylor University were especially helpful in the selection and production of the photographs used in this book. I am always mindful of Dr. and Mrs. Robert Walker, my wife's parents, in whose home I wrote this and several of my other books. Thanks must also go to Baker Book House, particularly Dan Van't Kerkoff and Betty De Vries, for their enthusiasm and confidence in this project.

I wish to remember my loving family: Jo Ann, to whom the book is dedicated, who at times must feel she is married to a book; and my three sons, Walker, Robert, and Preston, into whose lives I must do my best writing.

Prologue

In the Shadow of Ape

Man is the only creature who cannot drink and breathe at the same time.

The human body is an enigma. Its fifty trillion cells are quite ordinary, but when fully assembled they form a frame that seems more tabernacle than barn. Only the human body uniquely stands and moves fully erect, freeing deft hands to do mind's bidding. Alone among the creatures the human body is naked, not protected against storm and thorns, but designed for contact with other humans. Only the human body is uniquely suited to mate face to face, person to person. The human brain alone has a center for understanding and producing speech. The human body goes through a longer childhood and a longer life than animals. These and many more unique characteristics of the human body should make us pause and carefully consider the nature of the being who possesses it.

Charles Darwin was convinced that man's body bore the indelible stamp of a lowly origin. I think that the opposite is more the case. Our bodies speak of humanness, personhood, value, design, and meaning. There is no denying that we are a part of nature, but we are also uniquely above it. The Hebraic view of body, which stresses the unified nature of body and spirit, seems preferable to a demeaning materialism or a simplistic dualism. We are

13

separate from our bodies, and yet we *are* our bodies. In ordinary usage the phrase "human nature" refers to those psychological and spiritual aspects of ourselves that segregate us from the animal world, although we do not usually think of our bodies as specifically "human." In the Hebraic, holistic view of the person, considering the body as human makes sense. In holistic thinking there is a close relationship, though not an identity, between who we are and what the body is. The body is our outer self and the medium through which we can express our inner thoughts and feelings. The body is also a partner in shaping those thoughts and feelings.

In studying the enormous differences between human and animal bodies, we should recognize that similarities between humans and animals are also to be expected. The similarities, though, should not be used to mask the obvious differences present. Jacob Bronowski, an evolutionist with a special view of human nature, commented accordingly:

> . . . . the wonderful work on animal behavior by Konrad Lorenz naturally makes us seek for likeness between duck and the tiger and man; or B. F. Skinner's psychological work on pigeons and rats. They tell us something about man. But they cannot tell us everything. There must be something unique about man because otherwise, evidently, the ducks would be lecturing about Konrad Lorenz, and the rats would be writing papers about B. F. Skinner.[1]

If we have overlooked the uniqueness of the human body, as I believe we have, it has been because of an over-enthusiastic support of the theory of evolution and the consequent need to see humans as the progeny of apes.

1. Jacob Bronowski, *The Ascent of Man* (Boston: Little Brown and Co., 1973) pp. 411–412.

Consciously or unconsciously, our scientific culture has made selections, recordings, and interpretations of data based upon what is relevant to the theory of evolution. This subjectivity has caused scientists to miss or ignore the amazing uniqueness of the human body.

In the haste to find similarity between man and animal, frail bridges have been stretched between these distant natures. The examples of animal behavior often brought forward to challenge notions of human uniqueness seem grossly inadequate. A commonly used example is that religious behavior of human beings, particularly prayer, is merely a variant of stereotypical behavior in pigeons. In such behavior the pigeon engages in highly ritualized responses, even when the receipt of a reward bears no relationship to the bird's behavior. People do show stereotyped behavior, for example, when a baseball player engages in the same ritual prior to every trip to the plate. But human religion and prayer are so much more profound than such stereotypes. The complexities of human culture have been compared to the Japanese macaque's cross-generational transmission of food-preparation behaviors, which include the washing of sweet potatoes and the separating of wheat from sand by immersion in water. This may be impressive behavior, but it is not even remotely comparable to the magnificence of human culture. So-called political behavior has been ascribed to baboons, since they have been observed to form "coalitions" during unfriendly encounters. However, reducing politics to temporary baboon alliances mutilates the meaning of politics. The human preoccupation with jewelry and fashionable clothes has been compared to behavior in an orangutan, one of which was seen in a lab to put some lettuce on his head like a hat and to examine the effect in a mirror.

These examples are interesting, but they fail to equate

complex human nature to that of the animal world. What is needed today in the study of human nature is a straight-forward investigation of the evident differences between humans and animals. Theory should be a guide to re-search and data collection, not an obstruction to a mean-ingful analysis of data. The latter seems to have been the case with the theory of evolution and the study of human nature. The sciences need to be in a better position to ex-amine openly the uniqueness of the human body. If we find that theory stands against a legion of clear facts about the human uniqueness, and we fail to admit to the facts, then so much the worse for our scientific efforts.

Researchers today must admit to the puzzling existence of complex human anatomical and physiological features for which there are no gradual approximations in the animal world. The structural differences in the human spine, pelvis, foot, thermoregulatory mechanisms, and the brain's speech center are just a few examples of unique complexities that appear fully developed in the human be-ing. It is also a continuing question as to how some of the complex features of the human body evolved, when there is no clear-cut survival advantage to the attenuated ver-sions of a specific feature supposedly developing in evolu-tionary history. Many uniquely human features are only an advantage to survival in a fully developed form, often only in conjunction with other complex features of the body or brain. The human upright posture is a good exam-ple of a uniqueness based upon several skeletal, muscular, and circulatory changes, all of which must be present si-multaneously in order for upright stance and movement to occur. Many of the unique human features are even clear disadvantages to physical survival and are therefore not seen in the animal world. Changes in the human airway for speech and the nakedness of the human body are good examples of this.

The purpose of this book is to examine in detail the fascinating anatomical differences between humans and animals in order to appreciate how all of these differences are part of God's design for us as persons. We will be learning, for example, that man is the only creature who cannot drink and breathe at the same time. This is because no animal throat has the complex design of our own. The human throat exists fully developed only in man and speaks clearly of the gulf between humans and animals in the physical realm. The human throat would not offer a physical-survival advantage to an animal, but rather a clear disadvantage, since it is far easier to choke to death on food with a human throat. The function of the unique human airway revolves around personhood, since the human throat was designed for manufacturing the ingredients of a spoken language.

In the task of examining other differences between humans and animals, chapter 1 explores the uniqueness of the human face and its ability to show forth the individual personality. Chapter 2 examines the human skin and its nakedness. The purposes that naked skin serves in our development and emotional sensitivity are unusually important to us as persons. Chapter 3 describes the unique sexual features of the human body and their design for love relationships. The long, slow human-development process is discussed in chapter 4. The role of an extended and weak childhood is critical in the formation of personal interaction skills and for the transmission of human heritage and culture. In chapter 5 the uniquely erect posture of human beings is studied, along with its effect on freeing the hands for culture building. Chapter 6 describes the human brain and the four ways it differs from primate brains. Each of these differences is seen to contribute to human thinking and self-awareness. Finally, chapter 7 studies the aging process and the human body's amazing longevity. This longer life in the midst of pain and suffering seems to be the impetus for the human quest for meaning in life.

There are many similarities between human and animal bodies. These are due to our common Creator and the environment and survival needs that we share. The differences between human and animal bodies, however, were designed by God for us, who were created persons in the image of a personal God. We possess a body that is human, without whose uniquenesses we would fail to develop as persons or fail to express adequately our unique attributes as individuals. Imagine that you found yourself trapped inside a worm's body or a chimpanzee's body for several hours. Pardon the dualistic language for a moment. Your ability to be a person and express your personhood to others would be crippled by the body you possessed. In a worm's body you could perhaps crawl across a window and scribble some green slime message about who you really are. But you would probably be exterminated before finishing a single word. The chimpanzee's body would better serve for communicating your unique personhood, because it is so much more mobile and skillful than a worm's. But, lacking a speech center and a long attention span, you might have to beat a few chess champions in order to convince people that you were a special chimpanzee. Only with luck would anyone guess that you were in the chimpanzee's body. With the expertly designed human body, however, your personhood can find full expression and rein.

We must not fool ourselves into thinking that it is

merely the right combination of physical features that turns apes into men. Personhood does not simply emerge from the propitious union of arched feet, opposable thumbs, curved spines, naked skin, facial muscles, and speech centers, although personhood is developed and expressed to its fullest in such bodies. Animals are not persons, and they have no need for the unique features of the human body. This book will closely compare the human anatomy to animal anatomies, particularly the apes, which are referred to as our near relatives. It is not surprising that we differ from the amoeba, but the vast differences between human and ape are particularly meaningful in the understanding of our origin and purpose in life.

I had the impression after reading Jane van Lawick-Goodall's book *In the Shadow of Man* that I had learned most of the facts of importance about chimpanzees.[2] It took her over ten years to get the facts, but only a few hours were required for me to digest them. The same is true for other books on primates. Chimpanzees are rather simple creatures. They eat all day, show threatening and charging behaviors, and establish dominance patterns. They alternate between aggressive acts and gentle responses. They have an outstanding intelligence, for an animal. Chimpanzees may use simple tools and have been taught to use simple language symbols. They go through periods of female pink swelling and male mounting. Mothering is very important, even five or six years after birth. There is not much more to tell, really, except the small details. Monkeys and apes may appear to be having an exciting life, but nothing could be further from the truth. Close up, their lives appear repetitious, dull, and

2. Jane van Lawick-Goodall, *In the Shadow of Man* (Boston: Houghton Mifflin Co., 1971).

monotonous by human standards. For their whole lives these primates live in the same stretch of forest with the same group of companions, eating the same type of food. That is what primates—and, in fact, all animals—are all about.

But human beings are spectacularly more. I have a Ph.D. and years of study behind me, but alas, I know a mere fraction of what there is to know about my species, its individuals, or even myself. When I study human nature, I feel as if I am drawing facts out of a bottomless black hole, in both their number and their stubborn resistance to be understood. I am not being naive or egotistical when I say that animal nature is simple. My impressions are honest. When I study primate feeding behavior or sexual behavior, I know that I am dealing with complicated material. But I do not get the same falling-into-the-ocean feeling that I get when I study the whole person.

Even when I study just the human body, I realize that there is more in view than just muscle and bone. There is something very important here. The body tells of our special design, of our personhood, of our glory. Let us then move out of the shadow of ape and see our bodies in a new light. Let us examine the body that is human—the body human.

1 Face to Face

Man is the only creature who can bleed to death through his nose.

Face to face

It is interesting that a human is the only creature, with the exception of birds, who does not have to raise its head to make an utterance. Our erect posture guarantees an arrangement of the windpipe and vocal organs that permits us to talk while maintaining the normal head position. Picture a cow mooing or a dog barking. The greater the volume of sound the animal attempts, the higher it must elevate its head. The lonesome coyote is not howling at the moon but merely attempting to generate some volume. Human beings, though, can speak or sing without straightening the head and neck, thus enabling them to maintain a level, face-to-face conversation. Imagine the difficulty of talking to someone and having to elevate your head at every word. The suitor's marriage proposal would fly over the young maiden's head. Angry words would set forth from hostile lips, but the accompanying cold stare would be lost on the stars. Unlike animals, human beings have the capability to maintain face-to-face interaction. Such a difference from the animal world is important, because human faces are uniquely designed for the expression of personhood.

All of us find ourselves attracted to a beautiful or handsome face. The face is usually our first introduction to another personality. We may appreciate a man's rugged, muscular build, or a woman's figure, but there is something special about an attractive face. This fact does not slight the average-looking person (which most of us are), but it recognizes that we possess a keen recognition of order versus disorder, of beauty versus non-beauty. We have a similar reaction when we gaze upon a beautiful pastoral scene or stained-glass windows, or when we hear a special piece of music. The mental and emotional pleasure that we have at these times says that this is the way that things should be. There is meaning here. It is the same with our introduction to a person through the face. The face says that there is something holy here. Average-looking faces communicate the same thing. The beautiful or handsome face (or the kind or gentle face) is simply a clearer picture of the way things really are.

The human face is so important in our personal communication and interaction that it troubles us to have a serious conversation on the telephone and not be able to see the other person's facial reactions. It is disturbing when someone refuses to look at us as we debate our side of an argument. Monsters in the movies usually have badly distorted human faces, as do the "bad guys" in gangster films. Victims of burns or facial paralysis struggle emotionally with the difficulties that people have in relating to them as persons. The impediment of a scarred face to interpersonal relating can be overcome if we spend the time touching and interacting as persons, in spite of our first reactions. However, the body human was made with a uniquely designed face to more immediately and more intimately reveal personhood.

Of all the creatures in the world, the human being is endowed with the most complex face to present to the world.

Our facial muscles provide us with the most intricate system of facial expression. In addition, the unique features of the human face join with the facial muscles to produce highly individualized faces. Even the apes cannot match the communicative power of the human visage.

In recognition of the importance of the face, human beings have always labored to add cosmetically what was lacking in nature's work. The ancient Egyptians enlarged their eyes with a border of dark paint. They powdered with green copper dust below the eyes and lead dust above. Egyptian women stained their cheeks red and darkened their eyebrows. The Greeks, unlike the extravagant Romans, were interested in simplicity and purity, and therefore added only a bit of color to their cheeks and lips. Seventeenth-century European women lavished on heavy makeup in imitation of the exaggerated makeup of the theater. In our own modern culture, billions of dollars are spent every year on the material of which faces are made: soaps, creams, gels, powders, conditioners, astringents. Although some of these are for the body, most are for the face, the picture window of the soul.

One of the most revealing facts about the human face is that—of all creatures, as far as we can tell—only human infants mature rapidly in the eye-brain in order to fixate on human faces, long before their other visual abilities catch up. The infant seems programmed (by the age of four or five weeks) to recognize and prefer looking at human faces rather than any other object, particularly moving faces or faces with moving parts. We practically enter the world looking for a face to gaze upon. By three to four months of age, the mother's face is generally the preferred object.

There is a disturbing malady that suggests that the human brain has a special area devoted to facial recognition. In a disorder called prosopagnosia (from *prosopon*, face; *a*,

not; and *gnomon,* one who knows) the person cannot recognize familiar faces. The problem seems to be caused by
lesions of the underside portions of the temporal and oc-
cipital lobes of the brain. People with severe prosopagnosia cannot even recognize members of their own family.
A male patient, for example, when introduced to several
people, including his wife, does not recognize her until
she begins to speak. Monkeys seem to be able to recognize faces, and cells have been located within monkey temporal cortex that are sensitive to faces and different face
attributes. It should be clear that facial recognition is not
as important to monkey survival as it is to human survival
as persons.

The Individual Face

Unlike any other creature, we are individuals more than
we are a species, and our faces are superbly designed to
express that individuality. Each amazing human being
begins as a mere speck of dust. The ovum weighs one-
millionth of a gram. In conception the sperm adds a mere
five-billionths of a gram to the ovum. What magician's hat
could equal the unpacking of this tiny package into the incredibly complex human being? I never imagined the dust
of creation to be so miniscule.

Within the fertilized ovum is the beginning of the person, the individual. At conception each of us stands on the
charmed ladder of DNA, a double helix of nucleic acid
that, if uncoiled, would match a man's height. The rungs of
the DNA strand are sequenced patterns of bases, coded to
make the being a person—not any person but a particular
person. The coded instructions of the original fertilized
egg are copied and contained in every cell of my body, so
that each of my cells remembers its beginning and its goal.

So faithful is the reproduction of the original code that any one cell of my body could theoretically be "cloned" to produce a body genetically identical to mine. (This technology is not long from being available, but perhaps we should spend time cloning cows to our use before we Xerox men.) Of course, a cloned tongue cell (or whatever) would not be "me," since I am also a product of my environment. The intricate design in the genetic code is molded by complex events in life to shape the individual person, and the shaping never stops. The four and one-half billion people alive today began as DNA strands in their original fertilized eggs. The total weight of those four and one-half billion coded filaments needed to specify every unique human being alive today would be about one-fifteenth the weight of a postage stamp! That is the way to shame a computer microchip without mercy.

Unlike any other animal, the human being seems to possess the potential for great individuality, particularly in the face. Animals seem much less variable as individuals in their faces. Dogs may vary in terms of type of dog, *e.g.*, bulldog or collie, but all collies look and act very much alike. Humans, on the other hand, though much less variable between the racial types, are extremely variable between individuals. It is easy to see the relative homogeneity of the human body, even when observing racial differences. The human body may vary in color. Variability is also seen in body size, with the range from pygmy at four feet to Watusi at seven feet. This is not a large difference when compared to the variations in dogdom from dachshund to Saint Bernard. The physical similarity between the racial types is part of the body-human's design to maintain unity in mankind. Given how we respond to small differences in skin color, we certainly do not need more excuses upon which to build our prejudices! The unity of the human race may be important, but diversity between individual humans in some way is also important. And it is in the face and in personality characteristics where the greatest differences are to be found.

Within a species, animal faces seem to be reasonable facsimiles of each other. When all the variables of such aspects as hair color, nose size, cheekbone structure, brow size, area of face, and eye separation have been manipulated in the animal face, little seems to have changed. If we saw thirty foxes in a cage, or thirty buffalo, we would be hard pressed to distinguish and recognize each animal as different from the others, based on facial features alone. Even if we had the personality of a buffalo and had spent much time gazing into friendly buffalo faces, it seems unlikely that we would be able to separate the crowd into thirty distinct buffalo faces. A buffalo face is a buffalo face. Once you have seen a few dozen buffalo faces, you have seen them all. In the higher primates, particularly the chimpanzee, greater variability in facial features and expression is possible because of increased facial muscle complexity. But even when considering the chimpanzee, fifty or several hundred chimps in a cage would exhaust our ability to distinguish among them. It is not that we lack discrimination. *They* lack the variability.

Field anthropologists often learn to recognize individual monkeys and apes by face, size, and temperament. In Jane van Lawick-Goodall's *In the Shadow of Man*, which chronicles her work with chimpanzees in the wild, she includes pictures of many of the chimps she spent a lot of time observing.[1] She named them Worza, Mike, Leakey, Goliath, McGregor. The human names were chosen because a chimp would remind her of some particular man-

1. Jane van Lawick-Goodall, *In the Shadow of Man* (Boston: Houghton Mifflin Co., 1971).

nerism or facial expression of a human acquaintance. The naming and anthropomorphizing helped her discern, perhaps better than anyone else in history, the individual differences between dozens of apes. Whenever larger, shifting menageries of monkeys and apes have to be followed, individual identification becomes too difficult. Rhesus monkeys under study are often tattooed shortly after birth with large numbers on their chests to make individual observations in the wild possible.

On the other hand, consider the human being. Of the four and one-half billion human beings alive today, almost all could be distinguished from one another, with the exception of identical twins. So great is the human facial variability that we could single out each of the billions of human beings as different from any other. I would not remember every face or name, but I would know most certainly that this face is not that face. They are all different. You will think it is so remarkable if you see someone who looks somewhat like yourself, or when you watch an Elvis Presley or Michael Jackson look-alike contest. We consider these things unusual because it is so rare that two human beings who are not related would look so similar! In fact, even the look-alikes in the contests are only approximations. Without a doubt, the human face is the most remarkable vehicle for our individuality.

The Emotional Face

With very few exceptions, striated muscles (also called skeletal muscles) attach to and move our arms, legs, and other bones. Some skeletal muscle, however, is situated in the fascia under the skin, where it inserts into and moves skin. An example of this use of skeletal muscle is in the horse, which has many such muscles in its body to twitch the skin in spots and so drive away flying insects. But the human being, unlike any other animal, has a face composed almost entirely of such subcutaneous muscle, which moves skin rather than bone.[2] Rather than assisting us in twitching bugs, these delicate muscles form the facial slate on which the volumes of human expression are written. Paper-thin muscles are arranged at the chin and forehead and grouped around the orifices of the face, the eyes, nose, and mouth. These muscles make it possible for us to squint, smile, frown, purse our lips, wrinkle our nose, widen our eyes, and thus communicate on our fleshy, ever-changing mobile our surprise, pleasure, disgust, love, fear, and more.

In all, there are some twenty-eight paper-thin human facial muscles involved in developing facial expression. Most of them are arranged in pairs and are barely an inch long. Facial muscles are also involved in moving the lower jaw for chewing and biting and in moving the lips when talking and singing. Muscles that ring the mouth shape it into a circle to show surprise. Other muscles pull the corners of the mouth up or down or sideways. Muscles from the scalp pull the eyebrows up, wrinkle the forehead during surprise, and make the eyebrows slant during crying. Rings of muscles around the eyes change the shape of the eyes. Muscles around the nose act to compress or flare the nostrils. Muscles attached to the chest pull on the lower part of the face to express sadness.

Most of our eating muscles are attached to the back part of the face in front of the ears. From there they pull on the lower jaw and chin. If you put your fingers behind your

2. Davis R. Swindler and Charles D. Wood, *An Atlas of Primate Gross Anatomy: Baboon, Chimpanzee, and Man* (Seattle: University of Washington Press, 1973) p. 64.

temple while you make chewing movements, you can feel the movement of these large muscles. The bulk of the muscles of a gorilla's face is involved in the movement of the gorilla's massive lower jaw, turning it into a powerful crushing and grinding device. These facial muscles of the gorilla are so large that they extend from the jaw to the upper part of the skull. To provide more bony attachment for these large, powerful muscles, the male gorilla possesses a sagittal crest along the top of its skull. It seems as if a large part of the gorilla's skull serves as a home for the huge jaw muscles. But the gorilla has very little effective subcutaneous facial muscle.

Although the chimpanzee has more facial control than any other ape, most of its muscle control surrounds its large lips. Observe a chimpanzee in the zoo and see how marvelously the chimp moves its lips in eating and smacking and making faces at people. The control is amazing, though far short of the human's control over more important parts of the face for the expression of emotions. Given the range of movement in our tiny facial muscles, it is possible for the human face to make more than a quarter of a million facial changes. Only a person can do that. Only a person needs to!

The orangutan has exceptional facial control around the mouth and nose and poor control elsewhere. Nevertheless, by controlling its large lips, the orangutan produces a wide variety of facial expressions, most of them comical. The muscular changes, though they resemble a variety of human expressions, do not necessarily correspond to what the orangutan is thinking and feeling. As with the chimpanzee, the large mobile lips seem to play an important role in the communication of a limited number of signals.

The gorilla has been typecast for the "bad guy" role because of his brooding, ferocious-looking appearance. He has huge teeth enclosed in mighty, protruding jaws. The skull is immense, with the sagittal crest adding to the height of the males. At six feet tall and four hundred pounds, and with massive chest and arms, the gorilla's appearance does not at all fit its true nature, which is rather shy and gentle. As the young gorilla matures, its skull develops in a way that pushes the eye sockets from underneath the cranium to far out front. A sloped forehead and prominent brow ridges are the result. Large, forward-jutting jaws are also developed. The lower jaw of the adult gorilla is big, but it lacks a protecting chin, which is so distinctive and characteristic of the human face. Instead, there is a bony "simian shelf" that lies at the front of the jaw.

Though the gorilla's scalp is hidden beneath dense hair, it is capable of some brow movement in a number of contexts. Unlike Old World monkeys, gorillas and chimpanzees lower their brows and "frown" as an expression of threat. When threatened, the gorilla will fix its stare at the other animal, tilt its head downward, and purse its lips. During aggression, a gorilla or chimpanzee will raise and draw back its lips to expose the teeth, then tilt its head back to emit loud screams.

Chimpanzees, in general, have a larger facial display repertoire than gorillas. Chimpanzees are capable of a broad smile that usually does not indicate what it does in man. In the chimp it is a sign of fear or tenseness. Other chimpanzee facial expressions include the compressed-lips face, shown during aggression; the play face, in which the upper lip is drawn back and up and the teeth are exposed; the pant-hoot, which is an audible intake of breath; and the panting face, in which the lips are pursed and the

chimp is screaming or squeaking.[3] Most of the chimpanzee's communication with its face is with the muscles of
the mouth and is associated with vocalizations.

Chimpanzees and other primates also show more subtle
facial signals, such as staring. Sometimes a single stare or
change of direction of the gaze by a dominant chimp can
strike fear in every furry chest in the group. Many species
of primates have eyes that are a different color than the
surrounding skin, and this further emphasizes the stare.
Primates also yawn to reveal large canines and engage in
lip smacking, in which the lips open and close rapidly and
the tongue moves in and out. The latter is used as an ap-
peasement gesture and during grooming.

This amount of facial expression in higher primates is
very impressive when compared to other animals, which
show next to nothing comparable beyond exposing the
teeth. Yet this facial communication falls far short of the
human potential to express personality and feelings in
the face. Whatever the success of the primates' facial expressions, they certainly do not even remotely resemble
the nature of the messages we modulate on our sensitive
facial muscles. Primate messages are largely limited to
"I'm here," "I'm excited," "I'm afraid," "Get away!"

Another difference between human and primate facial
communication is in the nature of its neural control and,
therefore, its motivational basis. Human facial expressions are controlled through learning by the brain's cerebral cortex, even though human emotions are rooted in the
limbic system. Animal facial expressions, on the other
hand, are controlled by the limbic system. This fact would
explain the small range of animal facial expressions and
the observation that massive removal of a monkey's motor

---

3. Lawick-Goodall, *In the Shadow of Man.*

cortex does not affect its facial expressions. Human beings, though, with damage to certain areas of motor cortex
will suffer facial paralysis. Several years ago a student of
mine had a tumor removed from her right hemisphere and
consequently lost some control over the left side of her
face. If I concentrated on observing the right side of
her face, her expression appeared normal. The left side of
her face, though, appeared passive and immobile. The
limited range of limbic emotions in the nonhuman primate needs little facial paper for expression, whereas the
rich limbic-cortical-personal feelings of man need endless reams.

The Responsive Face

The Smile of Joy

There are two important facial expressions of the body
human not seen in any animal. One is the embarrassed
blush, which we will examine later. The other is the joyful
smile. Primates may look as if they are smiling, with their
lips drawn back and teeth visible, but that is always an expression of anxiety and fear. In humans the smile indicates
joy and mental and emotional pleasure. To smile is to be
human. A smiling face is beautiful to behold.

Smiling is a special expression related to, but not the
same as, laughing. In its mildest form a laugh is similar to
a smile, but the beaming smile is vastly different from the
hearty laugh. The inborn nature of the smiling response
shows that it is rooted deeply in what it means to be human. Babies will spontaneously produce smiles a few
hours after birth. Even blind babies smile. But unless parents reinforce a baby's spontaneous smiling by touching
or talking to the baby, the expression soon diminishes. By

the time an infant is four weeks old, it begins to smile at visual stimuli, with a moving face being the most reliable stimulus. Smiling is a personal, two-way street, since it has an incredible effect on the new parents. It has the same effect in adult relationships. We are so accustomed to looking at smiles that we fail to realize that it is one of the most complex, idea-filled expressions that a human being can deliver.

The Eyes

The gemstones of the face are the eyes, which are called the windows of the soul in the Bible. As windows they reveal so much of the life within that it would bother us to see a corpse with open eyes at a funeral, or a sleeping person who has an eye that will not close. The eyes squint, smile, stare, glow, glare, wink, gleam, and cry, communicating message after message from the person within. The child who is being scolded cannot look the parent in the eyes. When we are embarrassed, we shuffle our feet and stare at the floor rather than make eye contact.

We cannot fixate on both eyes when we look a person in the face. We each habitually gaze at either the left or the right eye. (I look at a person's right eye.) We are never aware of this phenomenon until we talk to a person with a false eye or an aberrant eye that stares off above our shoulder. We become disengaged when the nonfunctioning eye happens to be the one we normally look at. We are confused when this occurs, until we force ourselves to look at the nonpreferred eye, and then we rediscover the person.

At birth a baby's eyes are already two-thirds full size and will remain disproportionately large throughout childhood. The eyes are the body human's traps, designed to snare parents' hearts. "Beauty" in a woman is also par-

tially determined by the largeness of her eyes, and the cos-
metic industry takes advantage of this. The eyes will also
expand through pupil dilation. The dark pupil of the eye is
similar to a camera's iris in that it automatically dilates
and constricts in response to the existing degree of light.
When we are in a dark room, the pupil automatically expands to admit more light. If we move from there to full
sunlight, we will feel a sharp, momentary pain in our eyes,
because the muscles controlling the pupils have con-
tracted so rapidly, reducing the pupil to a pinpoint to protect our eyes from the sun.

The pupillary response of the eye is also controlled by a
variety of cognitive and emotional responses that have
nothing to do with light. Our pupils will dilate when we are
looking at good food, an interesting painting, or an attractive member of the opposite sex. Since the eye is also a window to the outside world, it opens widely to show us more
of what we want. Conversely, the pupils will constrict
when we are viewing something with disinterest or dislike.

These dilations in pupil diameters also serve to make
faces more attractive to us. Experiments have shown that
we are attracted more to photographs of people when the
pictures have been retouched to enlarge the pupils. Along
with smiling, pupil size and eye makeup serve the most to
make us attractive to people. We can be sure this is why
some Renaissance women put the drug belladonna in
their eyes, because belladonna enlarged the pupils. If we
understand this autonomic pupillary response correctly,
it appears that we are automatically attracted to people
who are attracted to us. Our eyes play matchmaker. I can
abandon pulling petals off flowers to see if she loves me. If
I am standing in a dimly lit room and staring into her eyes,
and I see that her pupils are a mere pinhole, she obviously
doesn't love me.

Facial Appendages

We will next examine the more prominent features of the human face, which give it character and individuality. The nose, earlobes, and outturned lips, which are absent or greatly reduced in the animal world, are important elements of the human face. Nature has not been as generous in providing animal faces with such large appendages as appear on human faces. Faces in the animal world are designed with heat loss in mind. Any appendages on a body, especially heavily vascularized ones, cause the organism to lose heat. Large noses and lips also run the risk of injury in the normal circumstances of running, feeding, or fighting. The question that then arises is why the human face differs from the animal's in this regard. We will see that the personhood advantage of large facial appendages outweighs the physical disadvantages of heat loss and potential injury.

The form of human and animal bodies reflects partial adaptations to climate and the problem of heat loss. The black race has adapted to a tropical climate with bodies that have proportionately long limbs and consequently a higher surface-to-volume body ratio, which helps dissipate unneeded body heat. This body form is present even in the pygmy. At the other extreme, the Eskimo's body is short-limbed and squat, resulting in a low surface-to-volume ratio. This body form aids the Eskimos in heat retention in their colder climates.

Even the faces of humans reflect adaptations to climate. To conserve heat, people living in the coldest regions of the earth, like the Mongoloid race, have faces designed to reduce the facial protuberances and thus the facial surface area. Mongoloid faces are relatively flat, with small noses, and they have cheekbones extended forward, eye sockets extended vertically, and reduced brow ridges. Such a face is also padded with fat, which gives it an even flatter appearance. What is unusual is that human faces in every climate have large noses and other extra protuberances such as earlobes and turned-out lips, which are disastrous for heat conservation. These peculiarly human features do not exist as such in the animal world, particularly the primate world, and biologists are left wondering about their purpose.

In asking the purpose of the human nose, it is interesting that man is the only creature who can bleed to death through his nose. Perhaps the most famous individual to die of a bloody nose was Attila the Hun. In A.D. 453 he returned to his Hungarian capital to add to his harem a young girl named Ildico. After a night of heavy drinking, Attila was found dead in bed beside his young bride. He had burst a blood vessel in his nose and choked to death as blood collected in his throat.[4] The reason that human noses can bleed so heavily is related to the nose's special design and purpose. When your mouth is closed, you can breathe entirely through your nose (barring any abnormality), since it is an efficient air vent. If the nose were nothing more than an air vent, one would not expect an external protuberance to be a part of the nasal structure. A whale, whose "nose" is just an air passage, has a single or double opening set flush with the top of the head. It is appropriately called a blowhole, since it can rapidly empty and refill the lungs with air.

Noses, though, are specialized instruments for many animals. The elephant's trunk is a highly useful arm and hand tool for feeding and bathing. In pigs the nose is thickened to form a rooting tool. Some moles have fleshy outgrowths for a nose, which then becomes an organ of touch

4. Will Durant, *The Story of Civilization*, vol. 4: *The Age of Faith* (New York: Simon Schuster, 1950) pp. 40–41.

to replace the eyes in the dark underground. But the human nose has none of these purposes to explain its lengthening past a vent hole. A longer nose does allow for more moistening and warming of the air, although this could be done entirely with longer air passages in the head. This is true of the nasal passages of the Mongoloid people who live in colder regions. Their nasal passages extend deeper to heat the air on its way to the lungs. The hairs in the nose, as well as its moist sides, serve to filter out dust particles and tiny insects, although this function could also occur entirely within air passages inside the head.

In response to climatic conditions, human noses do vary in size and shape. The Negroid nose, which is exposed to relatively warm, moist air, is short, with wide nostrils. In contrast, the Caucasian nose is longer and has narrower nostrils. This long, narrow passage aids in warming and moistening the cooler air. But never do we observe the absence of a nose in the normal human face. It dominates the appearance of the face and, more than any other feature, it creates a general impression of a person's looks.

The higher primates provide good examples of what our noses ought to look like, since we, too, do not need the moist, scent collectors and long snouts characteristic of most mammals. These primates are divided into two groups, the Platyrrhina (flat-nosed) and the Catarrhina (down-nosed). The former group includes the New World monkeys, which have flat noses almost flush against their faces. Their nostrils are well separated and open straight forward. This is actually no nose at all, just two round holes separated by a broad nasal septum. The Catarrhini are the Old World monkeys. This group includes the baboons and the apes. Their noses project a tiny amount, with comma-shaped nostrils close together and facing downward. One notable exception in the story of paltry monkey noses is the proboscis monkey, a comical Old World monkey. This appropriately named species of langur found in the forests of Borneo has a large, long nose occupying a full quarter of its face. So large is the nose that it has to be pushed aside for drinking. Since it is found only in adult males, it seems to be a sexual attractant and not a forerunner to the human nose.

The human nose, unlike animal noses, is heavily vascularized, and, therefore, severe nasal hemorrhaging is possible in humans. The side walls of the human nose are filled with a spongy erectile tissue similar to the tissue in male and female genitals. As in the genital erogenous zones, the nose becomes engorged with blood by vasocongestion during sexual arousal. The nose, therefore, has all the characteristics of an erogenous zone. During sexual arousal, the nose becomes highly sensitive to the tactile stimulation of nose contact during kissing. In addition, breathing tends to increase during arousal. Since the mouth is blocked by kissing and the nose passages are constricted by tissue swelling, greater airflow during this increased breathing further stimulates the nasal passages. Breathing becomes labored. I suppose teenagers in a parked car really do engage in "heavy breathing," as our language implies. The nose is certainly not the most important erogenous zone of the body human, but it is a splendid example of a physical difference in man that serves a personal purpose. The importance of face-to-face mating, prolonged foreplay, and personal communication in the human sexual response increases the usefulness of erogenous zones that are distant from the genitals and near the face.

Earlobes and outturned lips serve the same erogenous purpose in man. The fleshy protuberances of the earlobes are completely absent from animal ears. Though they may vary in length (it seems to be an inherited trait), we all have earlobes. As in the case of the nose, the earlobe seems to be a secondary erogenous zone with increased sensitivity during sexual arousal.

Another unique feature of the human face is the presence of sensitive, turned-out lips. Chimpanzees can, for short time periods, turn back their lips in an exaggerated pout, but the lips must soon return to their normal thin-lipped state. Unlike other animals, we have permanently everted, rolled-back lips. To chimpanzees we must always appear to be in a pout. Chimpanzees use their lips for a variety of communication signals, including a tactile greeting. Permanently exposing the sensitive inner portion of the mouth, however, is not an advantage to the chimps. To us, on the other hand, lips are another erogenous zone, designed for kissing. The sensitive lips are permanently exposed, making prolonged kissing easy. I suppose primates do not "French kiss" because they would then have to maintain special muscle contractions around the mouth.

The Speaking Face

Another unique feature of a human being's face is a protruding chin. No primate has a chin that juts outward. Since monkey and ape chins point inward and are supported by extra bone, the area available for muscles to move the tongue is reduced. The human's projecting chin, on the other hand, allows room for considerably more freedom for the tongue. Consequently, the number of sounds that an ape can make are much more restricted than in man. The chin is not just designed to add character to our faces; it is part of a larger design to support our speaking capabilities.

Amazingly, we are the only creature on the globe that

cannot drink and breathe at the same time. The reason is that the human throat is specially designed for speaking. In breathing or speaking, the vocal cords must be separated or open. In swallowing, though, the vocal cords shut tightly to protect the tracheobronchial tree from any food particles or liquid that may get past the epiglottic cartilage.

Human vocal cords are two small folds of mucous membrane stretched across the cavity of the larynx (the voice box). The larynx, whose large size in males is a secondary sexual characteristic, projects from the middle of the neck after puberty and is popularly known as the Adam's apple. The sound of the human voice is a product of the larynx in conjunction with the cavities of the mouth, throat, trachea, and lungs. The vocal cords within the larynx are made to vibrate by air expelled from the lungs. The nose, mouth, throat, and chest serve as resonating chambers. When we speak or sing, the vocal cords, which are normally relaxed, are drawn closer together. In men the cords are longer and thus the voice is deeper. All of us can change the length of our vocal cords to some extent and thus alter the pitch of our voice.

In human speech the sounds produced by the vibration of the vocal cords are modified by the changes in size and shape of the pharynx and the mouth. It is at this point that the difference between the human and the animal becomes obvious. Man's pharynx, the shape of the mouth, and the position of the tongue seem designed to produce the complexities of speech. Our simplest speech involves incredibly complex coordination of nervous pathways and the many muscles of the larynx, tongue, and lips.

Nonhuman primates possess supralaryngeal vocal tracts in which the larynx exits directly into the oral cavity. In the adult human the larynx exits into the pharynx.

Thus the human supralaryngeal vocal tract seems better adapted for speech production than any other function. The amazing human capacity to shape complex sounds arises from the dynamic properties of the vocal tract, acting as an acoustics filter. The human speaker can vary the sounds produced by the vocal tract by changing its length and shape. This occurs by altering the posterior position of the tongue, raising or lowering the tongue, raising or lowering the larynx, retracting or extending the lips, or by opening or closing the nasal cavity to the vocal tract.

When a child is born, and until approximately the age of two, its vocal tract is similar to that of all animals. After age two the vocal tract develops according to the adult design, conveniently by the same time that neural pathways in the brain are well developed for speech production.

These vocal-tract differences in the adult human would not be advantageous to any animal. The respiratory efficiency of the adult human's supralaryngeal airway is about one-half that of the newborn. The right-angle bend in the adult's supralaryngeal airway creates resistance to the flow of air.

In an animal's supralaryngeal anatomy the oral cavity can be sealed from the rest of the airway during inspiration. This aids the sense of smell and allows the animal to breathe and swallow a liquid at the same time. By contrast, I have trouble swallowing a large pill because I cannot breathe while I am drinking what seems like a gallon of water trying to get the pill down. A human's vocal tract is limited in that food lodged in the pharynx can block entrance to the larynx. This is not a problem in the animal world because the supralaryngeal pharynx serves as a pathway for both food and liquids; but it is only an airway in humans. Anyone who has choked on food will realize this clear-cut disadvantage in the human design. Considering these obvious disadvantages inherent in the human vocal tract, it is clear that the tract has been designed primarily for the communication needs and capabilities of the human being.

The neurophysiologists say that I am my brain. But I know better. More than any other part of my body, I am my face. If my face were badly disfigured in an accident, I would still be there. But I would be a little further away, pushed back into my body, cut off from my most traveled two-way street to the world. In the morning in front of the bathroom mirror, my face reminds me of who I am. During the day it introduces me to the world—not just "Here is an animal," or "Here is a human," but more than that. It says, "Here is Mark. He is kind. He is jealous. He is compassionate. He lacks courage. He is embarrassed. He is perplexed." As I age, my face changes, but most of the human message remains the same. Our faces are singular personalities. They are pictures of the way things really are, of the way human beings are, of the way we will always be. Each day for every person the face magnificently earns its place in the body human.

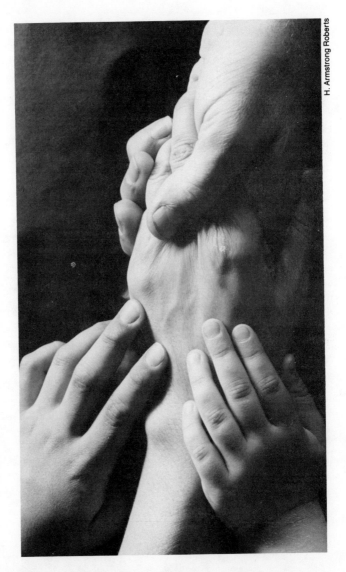

2 Feeling Is Skin Deep

Man is the only creature who keeps his cool by sweating.

If man is an ape, he is the only naked one. Of almost two hundred species of monkeys and apes, all have hair. Wherever we have a uniqueness in our bodies, it is there by design, God's design for personhood. The uniqueness of our naked, ultrasensitive skin is no exception. With our naked skin, we move into the human realm of enriched feeling, particularly emotion, which, among all our distinguishing features, so readily separates us from the animal world.

Lacking protective fur, our skin is exposed naked to the world. Skin is the largest organ of the body—some twelve to twenty square feet and 12 percent of our body weight—and it is certainly the most visible body organ. We give little thought to our skin until an unwanted splinter or rash or fiery sunburn seizes our attention. Human skin is soft and sensitive to help inform us, but it is also callous from use to protect us. Our bodies are 75 percent fluid, locked in by skin. Our internal organs are soft and vulnerable, guarded by skin.

Human skin is keenly sensitive, unlike the tough rind of the rhinoceros or the shell of the armadillo. Skin can bring us gentle contact with others, a light touch, a warm embrace. Though our skin is only matter, it is living matter, uniquely human matter as it joins with us in our deepest emotions. We tremble with rage, get hot with passion, turn cold with fright, or cool to another person. Our skin can crawl with revulsion. The body human's skin is a tabloid on which is headlined our innermost feelings and thoughts. We cannot stop the blush of embarrassment or the perspiration of anxiety, which are certain hints of the mind's fears.

The skin represents our appearance, our beauty or lack of it. As with the face, body skin is decorated to add what the double helix forgot. The Tiv people of the Benue Valley of Nigeria use razors and nails to lacerate their skin and then add charcoal or indigo to enhance the latticework of scars. To the Tiv this is beauty. The Nuba women of southeastern Sudan also practice scarification, creating patterns on the body that chronicle a young girl's passage to womanhood. A ferric-oxide antiseptic is applied to crescent-shaped wounds to form shiny, beadlike scars. The Suya tribe of South America stretches the skin of the earlobes with progressively larger disks until the lobes dangle to the shoulders. The lower lip is also distended in this way. The intended result is increased attractiveness and a visible exaggeration of the wisdom associated with listening and speaking.[1] Tattooing the skin like a painter's canvas is found the world over. Inert, metal-based pigments, which will not react with the body's chemistry, are inserted into the skin. The painting may be a masterpiece or a simple "I love Betty Lou."

Our skin is a multifaceted organ with three major layers and numerous subdivisions within these. The middle layer is the dermis (skin). It is bordered above by the epidermis (overskin) and below by subcutaneous tissue (underskin).

1. Doug M. Podolsky and the editors of US News Books, *Skin: The Human Fabric* (Washington, D.C.: US News Books, 1982).

The subcutaneous layer is an insulating, energy-storing cushion, protecting muscles, bones, and body organs. The dermis houses blood vessels, nerves, sweat and oil glands, and hair follicles. This layer consists largely of collagen, one of the strongest proteins in nature, and a lesser amount of elastin, a stretchable protein. Together these two proteins give the skin its durability and elasticity. The human scalp and face possess more elastin than collagen, which contributes to the amazing pliability for facial expressions. The outer layer of skin is only about one millimeter thick, no thicker than half a dozen sheets of paper. It is thickest on the hands and feet and thinnest on the eyelids.

The epidermis produces the fingernails, toenails, and hair. One unusual fact about hair is that it contains the largest inhabitant of the skin. Inside some of the hair follicles of the eyelashes, nose, chin, and scalp of most adults lives a wormlike mite called *Demodex folliculorum*. It lives its whole life in a hair follicle, deposits its eggs in a nearby oil gland, and journeys across the skin at night when in search of another follicle to live in. (If I think too long about this little skin mite, I find it harder to sleep at night.) What the mite eats or what role it plays in the life of the skin is still unknown. The epidermis also contains pigment and thus accounts for the color of one's skin, hair, and eyes. At the base of the epidermis, mitosis (cell division) occurs, providing millions of new skin cells every day. This process depends upon the body's available energy and therefore usually occurs between midnight and four A.M., when the body's other processes have slowed down.

The human skin exhibits a beautiful variety of colors, which, unfortunately, have often been the focus of prejudice and hatred. All human skin colors are the product of the same pigment, melanin. This dark pigment also gives the ripe banana and the leopard their dark spots. Two forms of melanin exist in our skin, hair, and eyes. Eumelanin is the major pigment, and it produces shades of brown and black. Phaeomelanin is the pigment of red hair. Differences in skin color are due to the varying amounts of melanin produced by the melanocytes that make up 1 percent of our skin cells. There are actually no red or yellow skin pigments. American Indians tan easily, which often gives them a ruddy color. Asians appear to have a yellow cast because the outermost layer of their epidermis, the *stratum corneum,* is thicker than that of Caucasians. This outer layer consists largely of keratin, which has a yellow tint to it. The Negroid race derives its beautiful skin color from a mere one-thirtieth of an ounce of melanin in the body. Think of building prejudice upon that!

Unfortunately, our skin is not perfect. It is vulnerable to injury and disease. Disfigurement to the skin is far more disturbing to the human personality than damage to any other organ except the brain. Perhaps the most bizarre of skin diseases is that of neurofibromatosis, or von Recklinghausen's disease, named after the German pathologist who first described it. The general public knew little about this disease until Ashley Montagu wrote the poignant book *The Elephant Man,* which depicted the life of Joseph Merrick, who was monstrously deformed by this disease. Joseph Merrick had deep personal needs for love and affection but was cut off from meeting them by his huge, misshapen head and wretchedly deformed body. The book, play, and later movie of *The Elephant Man* compassionately explored the man within his horrible bodily prison. The body is not the man, but it surely is an integral part of all that he is and must do. It is no wonder that the

Hebrew Scriptures taught about the unity of body and spirit that makes the living being.

Naked and Not Ashamed

There are over 4,200 species of mammals in our world and only a few are not covered with fur. We are one of those few, and the reason for our nakedness still eludes biologists. Desmond Morris, in his book *The Naked Ape*, puzzled over the nakedness of man in a world of fur and feathers and never arrived at a satisfactory explanation.[2] Only a handful of mammals (but no primates) are hairless or nearly so. They include the elephant, hippopotamus, rhinoceros, dolphin, whale, bat, pig, and some burrowing animals. In each of these cases of hairlessness, there is a good reason to be found. Elephants, hippopotamuses, and rhinoceroses possess few body hairs because of a heat problem. Along with their large size they have a large volume-to-surface body ratio and consequently relatively less body surface to dissipate body heat than smaller animals. Hair would be a disadvantage to such a very large mammal. Whales, dolphins, and porpoises are swimming creatures, streamlined for rapid movement in the water. Fur would serve no advantage, and insulating blubber makes up for the heat loss in cold water. Pigs and a few burrowing animals (the naked mole-rat, the aardvark, and the armadillo) have a greatly reduced hair covering. Moving around in the dirt presents a problem with cleanliness. Although furred animals keep conspicuously clean, it is probably asking too much of a pig's tongue to groom the dirt and mud from its body. The bat, which is the only fly-

2. Desmond Morris, *The Naked Ape* (New York: Dell Publishing Co., Inc., 1969).

ing mammal, is designed for lightness, and fur would be unnecessary weight. Therefore, its wings are naked.

But why are humans naked? We are not large animals. We neither live in the water nor burrow underground. And we do not fly. All of the normal predictors for nakedness in a mammal fail to apply to humans. There are halfhearted attempts at explanations, however. Perhaps we went through an aquatic phase in our evolutionary past and lost our hair, with the exception of that on the top of our heads, which protected us from sunburn when our heads were above water. There is no evidence for such a past aquatic phase for human beings except that we are the only creature with a layer of fat beneath the skin like a whale's blubber. Perhaps we descended from the trees and became carnivores. Racing after game on the hot savanna plain, as opposed to living in shady forests, would have caused us to overheat. But, if this is the case, then why are not lions and other carnivores also naked? Nakedness is not essential for the hunter or the hunted. Another theory proposes that the discovery of fire and clothing made hair expendable. But why would humans put on clothes and sit near a fire if they were already warmed by fur? This theory surely has things backwards.

Hair might have hindered the ability to see human facial expressions of anger or affection. But most primates possess less facial hair, presumably to reveal more facial expressions. There would be no need to bare all. Interestingly, the human male still has hair on his face, chest, and pubic area, where primates tend to lack or be thin on hair. Some theorists even suggest a solution to the question of our nakedness by saying that we are not really naked. We do have roughly as many hairs per square inch on our body as primates, although most of a human's body hair is so fine that it is all but invisible to the naked eye. But our body hair is hardly a thick mat of fur hiding the skin. This theory sounds like a reversal on the old "The King Has No Clothes" story.

Therefore, the question remains. Why are we naked? What was the supposed evolutionary advantage of nakedness? Our naked skin provides less protection against injury, no camouflage, no weapons, no defense, and no warmth. It is not that our bodies cannot grow hair. We have a lot of hair for very specific functions. Eyebrows keep sweat out of the eyes. Eyelashes warn the eyes to close if dust strikes them. Tiny hairs in the ears and nostrils act as filters for airborne particles. Hair in the armpits and pubic area may function as dry lubrication or as a scent catcher. Each body hair also contributes to the sense of touch, since a bare neuron surrounds the root of each hair.

The major disadvantages of nakedness in man are two: exposure to dangerous ultraviolet radiation and the problem of heat loss. Some exposure of the skin to ultraviolet radiation from the sun is needed because this radiation converts a type of sterol in the skin into a form of vitamin D, which is essential to the proper development of bone. The dangers of ultraviolet radiation to the skin, including skin cancers, are countered somewhat by the skin's increased production of melanin in sunlight. Exposure to the sun, therefore, usually results in a tanned skin, which acts as a protective filter against future ultraviolet bombardment. Light-skinned, blue-eyed individuals (hair and eyes also owe their color to melanin) with little melanin production seem to burn regularly but never tan. Light-skinned individuals often produce melanin only in localized spots of tan called freckles, which seem easily formed by those whose light hair also contains a reddish pigment. Tanning, though it partially protects the skin, has its disadvantages later in life. Premature wrinkles, sags, dis-

colorations, and a leatherlike skin are its results. Constant
exposure to the sun can cause more serious damage in that
the ultraviolet radiation in the sun can cause lethal as well
as mild forms of cancer.

The other disadvantage to the nakededness of human
skin is the problem of heat loss. Generally, the larger an
animal, the smaller the relative surface area of that animal
in relation to its volume. Thus, it is easier for large animals
to remain warm. For this reason, polar animals tend to
come in king size (polar bear, walrus, musk-ox). Children
are usually colder than adults, since they have more relative body surface to radiate heat away. Smaller animals
also have to eat proportionately more to replace the energy
lost at the body's surface. The tiny shrew, the smallest
mammal, must eat continually or die. The bottlenose dolphin, about the size of a man, must consume twice as
much as a human because of its problem with heat loss
in extremely cold water. This is also why a cat, at one-
twentieth of my weight, needs more than one-twentieth of
my meal to survive.

Why, then, are we naked, given that there is no obvious
biological advantage and several serious disadvantages to
naked skin? The answer is to be found in the design of the
human body with personhood in view. Our body is more
human than animal. A careful study of the human body
and its skin shows that our skin is far more sensitive than
the skin of all other mammals. This greatly expands the
range of human experience, particularly sexual experience. In addition, contact with the skin of the developing
infant is critical to the life and personal development of
the child. Finally, the naked human skin is important to
our rich experience of emotional feeling, a richness that
animals must surely lack.

Skin and Sensitivity

The sensitivity of human skin is incredible. Skin is sensitive at every location on the body, so as not to miss any stimulus. Skin sensitivity is highly refined at birth, while the other senses lag behind. The skin is populated by legions of tiny detectors with strange shapes—such as onions, eggs, disks, lacework—and with stranger names: Pacinian corpuscles, Meissner's corpuscles, Merkel's disks, Ruffini endings, and Kraus end bulbs. These receptors reside in the skin, shallow and deep, wrap around hair roots, wedge into joints, congregate in the lips, tongue, hands, feet, and genitals—reporting hot, cold, pain, and pressure. We are baffled about the origin of such experiences as pleasure, itch, or tickle. It must be that all sensory information is combined with the rich volume of human expectation, memory, and attention to produce our complex tactile experiences.

Because our skin is naked and exposed, it makes direct sensory contact with the world. Each sensitive capsule or free nerve ending touches the world directly, not through a thick, furry pelt, but through the soft, pliable skin. The faintest breeze, the softest touch, and the smallest raindrops will initiate depolarizations in the skin's neural network and thus begin the fabric of experience. A mosquito lands on my hand, and, before she can anesthetize my skin, I flick her away. The breeze bends several hairs on the back of my hand, and I may think a mosquito is there.

There is little research available on the sensory capabilities of mammalian skin. Superior sensitivity in visual, auditory, and olfactory senses is understandable in an animal's world of survival. Skin sensitivity, though, is not the highest requirement for a mammal's survival. But, even if human and animals' skin receptors were comparable in number and sensitivity, sensing the world through a fur coat must surely diminish the experience. It is also inconceivable that the sensory system of animals in the wild uses valuable neural sensors to process information unrelated to survival. Food is important. The cool summer breeze is not. The body human, on the other hand, seems designed to reveal much more of the subtleties of tactile experience, largely in the form of pleasurable physical experiences.

In addition to being naked, human skin is more vascularized than animal skin, resulting in heavier blood flow to the surface of the body. This increased blood flow makes the Caucasian, whose skin is actually white, appear pinkish or "flesh colored" because of the tint that the red blood gives to the skin. With increased blood flow to the skin surface, more sensory and neural activity is possible, increasing the skin's sensitivity. Whenever blood flow is cut off from the skin, such as when we cross a leg under ourselves while sitting, numbness results. Animal skin must feel slightly numb all of the time.

One major reason for the naked design of the body human is the increased sensory experience available in human sexual love. The human sex act, by virtue of its face-to-face position, is a massive, whole-body, tactile experience. Human mating is not brief genital-to-genital contact, but a longer skin-to-skin experience at the peak of tactile sensitivity. The human sex act involves carnal knowledge, or fleshy knowledge. It is usually preceded by a casual touch on the forearm, a hug, an uncertain first kiss, a hand-in-hand walk on the beach, a caressing, a hungry, passionate kiss. The Song of Solomon described marital love in poetic beauty. The words create in the reader the tactile images of sexual love as the lover caresses the beloved's body, runs his fingers through her hair, and kisses her lips. Much more of the world of love and sex is opened up to us because of this bare skin we have been given—and that we can give to another.

Skin and Life

The importance of skin contact during development in primates was shown very convincingly by psychologist Harry Harlow. He found in his experiments that Rhesus monkeys, isolated soon after birth and raised with surrogate mothers made of wire, did not become socially mature as adults. They sat for long periods of time staring blankly into space and reacted to stress by hiding and screaming. They engaged in self-mutilating behavior by pinching their skin between their fingers. Later they were extremely antisocial and had difficulty mating. As mothers they lacked warmth and affection and occasionally killed their young. Monkeys raised with a soft-cloth surrogate mother, on the other hand, spent most of their time in close physical contact with the cloth-covered "mother." These monkeys developed normal social and mothering patterns of behavior. The results with cloth mothers showed that contact comfort is very important to primate development.

Close physical contact has also been shown to be important in the development of the human being. Given the complexity of the social and personal patterns of behavior in a human being, it is understandable that contact comfort is even more important to human infants. If physical contact with parents is crucial to development, it is an important design feature of the body human that a baby's skin is naked. On bare skin the sensations of touching and handling by the parents would be greatly magnified. The importance of touch to the infant has been evidenced by the high infant-mortality rates in some orphanages and hospitals. These high death rates disappeared when frequent physical contact with babies was routinely required.

Close physical contact with autistic children has been shown to be helpful for these apparently stimulus-starved youngsters, who are continually hitting or mutilating themselves. Therapists also report that massaging, caressing, and embracing are important in the treatment of many schizophrenic patients. One of the more remarkable cases of recovery from the personal isolation of being raised by animals was a case where daily massaging was employed. Kamala, the wolf girl of India, was raised by wolves until she was eight. When rescued she refused to

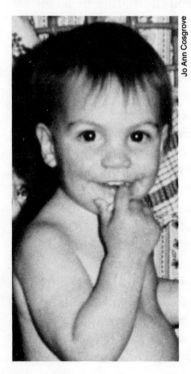

Jo Ann Cosgrove

Touching bare skin is vital in child development.

wear clothes, walked on all fours, and continually caught chickens in the yard and devoured them on the spot. Finally, her caretakers began to spend more time with her in tender massages. It was hoped that the daily massages would loosen her muscles and bones for more human use. As the circulation in Kamala's body extremities improved, she gradually learned to walk upright. What is more remarkable was that in spite of being recovered at so late an age, she began to acquire humanness. She learned to wear clothes and to prefer the company of people to dogs and cats. (See chapter 4 for further discussion of feral children.)

The connection between skin contact and a child's personal development is the human brain. Necessary and optimal brain development seems to depend upon the touching of the baby's skin. Imagine that! Our marvelous computer brain, which holds all the predisposing programs for human development, has its final wiring and final programming done through the skin. The skin is the terminal by which messages are sent to and received from the brain. The skin is an extension of the brain exposed to the world. The skin is an extension of ourselves.

Whenever we caress our child's neck or arms, or whenever we rough-and-tumble wrestle on the carpet, thousands of neural signals, electrochemical messages, move upwards toward the brain at a hundred meters a second. When these messages arrive, they apparently provide the energy and activity to move brain construction toward completion. The infant's brain grows until age two, and complicated interconnections of neurons are formed for several more years. Bare skin in the infant is an invitation to something important. Not one small touch will be lost because a coat of hair intercepted it. All sensation is welcome, is sought after, is coveted. The naked newborn is poised and ready when the physician delivers the first slap on its skin.

A connection between the lack of early skin contact and later human violence is a possibility. It seems that any type of body movement and skin contact sends trains of neural impulses to the cerebellum, which is the part of the brain important in the coordination of movement. Minor damage to the cerebellum might leave one unable to move a pen or shoot a basketball. The cerebellum is a unique part of the brain in that it is the only part of the brain where cell multiplication and growth continues long after birth, for at least two years. When an infant is rocked or touched, this provides direct stimulation for cerebellar development. The lonely rocking behavior of isolation-reared monkeys or institutionalized children may result from a lack of sufficient movement and tactile stimulation.

It is difficult to gather conclusive evidence to connect the cerebellum to emotional development, but there are some interesting leads. Movement and gentle physical stimulation are emotionally soothing to us. We rock in chairs, get massages, even stroke our own skin. Male chimpanzees often attack or threaten subordinates, but then they are quick to calm the victim with an embrace or touch of reassurance. When chimpanzees are nervous, they come together and touch each other for reassurance. When they spot some bananas, they kiss and embrace to celebrate their good fortune. Emotions are obviously related to the sense of touch in these experiential examples. The method of evoked potentials (electrically stimulating one part of the brain and checking for activity in another) has shown connections between the cerebellum and parts of the brain related to emotional expression. In addition, autopsies of the brains of monkeys reared in isolation reveal structural damage to the cerebellum.

It is reasonable to suggest that a lack of close physical contact in the early years of a child's life may result in inadequate emotional development. It is no accident that child abusers often come from child-abusing and affection-starved backgrounds. Child abusers resemble Harlow's monkeys in their inability to show physical affection. And the sin of abuse may be passed from parent to child, from skin to brain to the next generation.

It seems interesting that a lot of our social problems might be partially alleviated if we would do what we have been physically designed to do. Skin contact is pleasurable. Babies are cute, and it is fun to wrestle with our children. Each touch is contact for life, for humanness, through the courtesy of the naked human body.

Skin and Emotions

Another way in which a sensitive skin is an advantage to a human being is in the area of human emotions. When we feel something emotionally, our skin reacts; and when our skin reacts, we feel the emotion more deeply. An example of the skin's connection to emotions is in sweating. We sweat in response to heat, but we also sweat when we are under stress. This may be the origin of the expression "the heat's on" when referring to pressure. A person in a rage turns red in the face and actually feels warmer, and we talk about his being "hot under the collar," or we say, "Don't get all burned up about it!" There is an emotion, a bodily response, and the feeling of that response all connected to each other.

It has been said that humans are the only creatures who blush or need to. Animal bodies are unable to shunt to the skin surface the volume of blood necessary for blushing. Nor do animals have sufficient self-awareness or cognitive

appreciation of environmental events to become embarrassed. The Hebrew prophet Jeremiah accused the people
of forgetting how to blush, when they became so comfortable with sin that nothing shocked or embarrassed them.
We might consider occasional blushing as a sure sign of
humanness, since it speaks of sensitivity, morality, and order. To lose this is to enter the blank, neutral world of the
animal mind.

Blushing, or reddening of the face, is the result of increased blood flow to the skin surface of the face and
sometimes of the neck and upper chest. Women blush
more than men. The blind blush. All races, including
blacks, blush. In Negroids the skin tint changes slightly or
becomes more black. Charles Darwin considered blushing
uniquely human. "Blushing," he said, "is the most pecu-
liar and the most human of all expressions."[3] Some monkeys will flush red, however. For example, the vakari
monkey, a rare, cat-sized monkey in the Amazon River area
has a face that is normally a rosy pink but turns crimson
during excitement or anger. But blush it does not.

The skin, as an extension of the brain, reveals the
cognitive-emotional life of the human. But the opposite
is also true. The body's peripheral responses during emotions can deepen the emotional experience.

In addition to the somatic nervous system, which controls skeletal muscles, we possess an autonomic nervous
system (ANS). The ANS is concerned with the control
of smooth muscle, cardiac muscle, and glands. Smooth
muscle is found in the skin, in blood vessels, in the eye
(controlling pupil size), in the gut, gallbladder, and urinary
bladder. When we are under stress—for example, when in
heavy traffic or when a neighborhood dog attacks us—the

3. Charles Darwin, *The Expression of Emotions in Man and Animals* (Chicago: The University of Chicago Press, 1965).

sympathetic division of the ANS automatically prepares our bodies for "fight or flight." The major sympathetic responses are increased heart rate, breathing, blood flow to the skin and muscles, and sweating. The interesting thing about human ANS function during this stress response is that it can be activated by thoughts and emotions and not just actual car accidents and knife attacks. Therefore, we may blush, sweat, catch our breath, overheat, and feel tight muscles during an emotional crisis.

An early attempt to explain feelings of emotion as feedback from the peripheral effects of the autonomic nervous system and from skeletal muscles was the James-Lange theory of emotions. Proposed independently by William James and Carl Lange in the late nineteenth century, this theory said that our emotions were *nothing but* our awareness of our body's peripheral responses. In the classic example of William James, if we meet a bear in the woods unexpectedly, instead of saying we are trembling because we are afraid, we must say we feel fear because we are trembling. In other words, the feeling of trembling *is* the feeling of fear.

This theory cannot be totally correct. William Cannon in 1927 observed that emotional states begin sooner, last longer, and are more varied than the body's autonomic responses. In addition, autonomic changes due to drugs do not by themselves produce emotional changes in people. Finally, when peripheral feedback is removed during paralysis, humans and, to a lesser extent, animals still exhibit emotional responses.

But Cannon's analysis does not totally destroy the James-Lange theory. In experiments involving the administration of adrenalin (under a fictitious name) to subjects, the drug's effects of increased breathing and muscle tenseness did confuse the subjects as to what emotions they were feeling. Observations of quadraplegic humans (who can receive no peripheral feedback about their bodily states) do show some differences in their emotional experiences. For these patients the intensity of their emotional experience is related to how high the spinal transection is. The higher the break, the less is the feedback, and the lower is the intensity of the emotions. The quadraplegics' comments concerning their emotional experiences are interesting. "I sit around and build things up in my mind, and I worry a lot, but it's not much but the power of thought."[4] The following is from a paralyzed man, who was fishing when his boat was sinking. "I knew I was sinking . . . I was afraid all right, but somehow I didn't have that feeling of trapped panic that I knew I would have had before."[5] Another paralyzed person said, "I yell and curse and raise hell . . . but it doesn't have the heart to it that it used to. It's a kind of mental anger."[6]

From all that scientists can discern, human emotion is a complex experience, involving primarily the cognitive life of the person and the central regions of the brain, particularly the hypothalamus, amygdala, and septum. But the richness of the emotional experience, especially in strong, sudden emotions, is contributed to by feedback from the body to the brain. Because of the increased blood supply to the skin and the extreme sensitivity of the skin, the periphery of the body human detects changes in the body due to emotional feelings and reverberates them back to the brain. Our emotional experiences, therefore, take on an added dimension and meaning, both to our pleasure and displeasure.

    4. Neil R. Carlson, *Physiology of Behavior,* 2nd ed. (Boston: Allyn and Bacon, Inc., 1980) p. 506.
    5. Ibid.
    6. Ibid.

Animals experience emotions such as rage, excitement, fear, and contentment. But compare their list with only this partial listing of human emotions: determination, joy, exaltation, love, adoration, heaviness, dejection, misery, gloom, fright, compassion, revulsion, loneliness, sexual arousal, envy, jealousy, humility, hostility, yearning, enthusiasm, maternal love, confidence, trust, abhorrence, nostalgia, gratitude, astonishment, depression, shame, elation, and so on.

The Skin in the Heat and Cold

There are some highly unusual thermoregulators in the animal world. Whales, as homeothermes (warm-blooded), face particular problems of heat loss associated with their cold-water environment. The rate of heat loss in whales is much greater than in land mammals because heat conductivity in water is almost twenty-seven times as great as in air. Therefore, the whale must have some sort of protection against heat loss. A layer of blubber is the whale's answer. In whales, as in hogs, a layer of blubber is located in the subcutaneous skin tissue. In this tissue are large conglomerations of fat cells and very little blood supply. White whales possess fifty to seventy centimeters of blubber, whereas sperm and humpback whales average twelve to eighteen centimeters. The blubber's thickness also varies in different regions of the body.

The opposite problem, that of living in a hot environment, is dealt with effectively by the camel which manages to survive for long periods of time without water. As much as we would like to believe otherwise, the camel does not store water in its hump. Neither the hump nor any of the chambers preceding the stomach function as water-storage tanks. Nor does the camel oxidize fat stored in the hump to produce water. Such an oxidation process would require additional oxygen through breathing, and more water vapor would be lost through respiration than would be gained by oxidation. The hump functions instead as a reservoir of metabolic energy. What the camel does to preserve water in its body is to carry a fever. The daytime core temperature of a camel may exceed 104 degrees Farenheit. This conserves water because the heat gained during the day would ordinarily have to be dissipated immediately by the evaporation of water. Instead, the camel loses heat by conduction and radiation during the cooler night. The camel uses only a small amount of water by evaporation from the skin and in the respiratory tract, in the urine (which is highly concentrated), and in the feces (which are exceptionally dry).

On a hot day a dog can chase a rabbit until the rabbit dies from overheating of the brain. This is because the dog (and also the sheep, goat, and cat) has the additional capability, unlike the rabbit and most mammals, to cool its brain and thus keep the brain's temperature, to a limited extent, independent from that of its body. In a network of blood vessels at the base of the brain, cooler venous blood from the dog's mouth and nose area lowers the temperature in the carotid arteries before it enters the brain.

At the smaller end of nature, insects habitually exposed to the extreme cold lower the freezing point of their body fluids by secreting an antifreeze called glycerol, similar to antifreeze in a car.

The supreme thermoregulator on the planet, though, is the human being. In the cold our body generates metabolic heat in skeletal muscles by synchronized tremors known as shivers. These shivering tremors, which occur at ten to twenty per second, generate heat to warm the internal organs. Animals can shiver, but babies under six months of age cannot. Therefore, cold is a threat to an infant's life.

What animals cannot do in the cold that man does so well is to move blood away from the surface of the skin. Blood is shunted away from surface capillaries and back into venous return channels called anastomoses. The body extremities may turn blue, but valuable heat from the body core is not lost to the cold atmosphere. The cool venous blood from the skin surface is returned predominantly by the *venae comites*, which are deep pathways running next to arterial vessels. This close proximity of venous to arterial vessels allows a countercurrent heat exchange to take place. In this exchange, heat from warm arterial blood flowing to the surface is passed to cool venous blood as it moves back to the body core. This efficient countercurrent heat-exchange system is also found in penguins, which lose very little heat, even though their feet are in almost constant contact with the ice.

Humans are also the only creatures to possess a layer of fat beneath the skin to insulate them from the cold. Specialized adaptations to the cold are seen very well in the Eskimos, who have a surface-to-volume body ratio designed for the cold regions of the north. The short, squat Eskimo body offers less surface area for the dissipation of heat than that of a tall, thin man of the same weight. Eskimos also have fewer sweat glands on the body than does the average human, with the exception of the face, where they possess more. Sweat glands on the face allow the Eskimo to dissipate heat from the only uncovered surface on his body. Eskimos also have a metabolism that is higher than normal because of their diet high in fish. The marvelously inventive Eskimo has also made some unique adaptations in clothing, such as waterproof birdskin undershirts.

In the heat we reveal our superiority as thermoregulators. The body human dissipates heat through blood flow to the bare skin and through sweat glands. With a circulatory capability not found in any other animal, we shunt blood into the tiny capillaries of the skin and eliminate body heat by radiation and conduction. Elephants and desert rabbits use their big ears as radiators in the same way, but only man shunts blood to the whole skin. During extreme heat, blood flow on the skin may be a hundred times the minimum, and therefore we flush red in hot weather. In hot weather, unlike the cold, most of the blood returns to the core of the body through the superficial veins, which process allows for continued heat loss to the environment.

Eliminating body heat by simple radiation is not efficient, particularly in hot weather. The human body is therefore continually moving water to the surface of the skin, where it evaporates. The conversion of water into water vapor utilizes the heat of the skin and thus cools the body. Since this moisture of the skin is invisible and the skin is dry to the touch, it is known as insensible perspiration. It flows from the sweat glands or diffuses directly into the skin from the underlying tissues.

Visible sweat, a dilute salt solution, appears when the environmental temperature increases. This sweat flows copiously from almost two million sweat glands distributed over the entire body. These sweat glands, which are unique to humans, are tiny coiled tubes in the dermis that draw fluid from the blood to form sweat. The tube of the sweat gland opens upon the surface of the skin and is called a pore. If the humidity of the atmosphere is high, the rate of evaporation declines and sweat collects on our bodies. When we see a lot of sweat on the body, the liquid is not vaporizing and body heat is not being lost. Therefore, we complain about being uncomfortable when the humidity is high. With copious sweating, a person may lose three gallons of water a day. In very humid weather this can be dangerous, since water is being lost without any cooling effect on the body. The effectiveness of sweating for thermoregulation was shown convincingly more than two centuries ago, when Sir Charles Blagden entered a chamber heated to 260 degrees Farenheit. Though this temperature was hot enough to fry a steak, his body temperature remained close to normal.

Unfortunately, sweat has a bad reputation, mainly because there are two types of sweat glands in the skin. The eccrine glands are the thermoregulators and release almost pure water. The apocrine glands, on the other hand, are a sexual characteristic, becoming active during sexual maturation. Located in the armpits, the ear canals, nipples, and around the genitals, they respond not to heat, but to strong emotions. Responsible for a billion-dollar deodorant industry, apocrine sweat is fed upon by bacteria that live in the skin, and a strong odor results.

In some mammals, such as dogs and cats, sweat glands are normally found only on the pads of the feet. A horse will sweat from large areas of its body surface, but this sweating is in response to stress, not heat, and is not very effective in controlling the horse's temperature. Many animals, such as the dog, thermoregulate in a way similar to sweating. They have evaporative heat loss because of air movement over moist surfaces of the mouth and upper respiratory tract. Rapid, shallow breathing (panting) and increased salivation serve to keep the dog cool. In extreme heat a dog may pant 200 or 300 times per minute and a bird 600 times per minute.

But no animal has the marvelous thermoregulatory capabilities of humans. Our naked skin is turned into an advantage through blood-flow and sweat-gland mechanisms. There is no gradual development of these thermoregulatory capabilities from lower animal to man, and monkeys and apes are rather poor thermoregulators in general. It is all part of nakedness and the design for personhood in the body human.

3 Sex as If People Mattered

The human female is the only female creature who can have an orgasm.

The most surprising differences between human and animal bodies become obvious when studying sexual activity. The body human tells us very clearly about the importance of our relating as persons in the act of sex. Our culture, on the other hand, has emphasized the animalism of sex at the expense of its personal features. The supposed "naturalness" of the animal act of sexual intercourse has been used as an argument against those who would support faithful marital sex rather than carnal promiscuity. To deny one's sexual urges has been made to seem unnatural. A close look at nature and the human body, however, suggests a strong personal dimension to human sexual relations. The human sexual response is designed by God for the pleasure and communion of persons.

The body human is designed to allow us to make love face to face, person to person, with prolonged whole-body contact. Human bodies are freed from the enslaving cycles of heat and ovulation to follow the commands of personhood, love, fun, and spirit. The human female is a joint partner in the sex act by the very nature of her body's unique design. She is not just nature's womb in which to plant the seed, but she is an equal partner in the motives, the pleasures, and the communication that is sexual.

Perhaps the mystery of the union of a man and a woman is greater than any of us can know in this life. But we can be sure, as we study the body human, that we have been placed outside the backdrop of animal procreation without losing the joy and pleasure of sex. We can enter into the physical act of sex and, by design, can simultaneously exist a dimension apart from the physical. We can see new perspective and meaning in the physical act of procreation. But we can also look with hope into things only hinted at in the abiding personal union of the marriage bed—two people, yet one, centered on the other, yet never losing sight of self.

Face to Face

A human is the only creature who, as a rule, mates face to face. Nowhere in the world is ventral-dorsal (front-back) sex the usual practice for human beings. This is not to say that there is anything wrong with sexual positions other than face to face, but rather that the face-to-face position is anatomically and psychologically natural for human beings, though not for any animal. Almost all of the erogenous zones of the human body are in the front, whereby frontal contact produces maximal stimulation. These areas include the lips, nipples, breasts, and genitals. Even the growth of hair around the genitals at puberty hints at the human design for face-to-face mating. Such hair functions as a dry lubricant to minimize the friction during frontal mating.

In the four-legged animals, the amount of body contact in ventral-dorsal mating is small, because these animals have relatively narrow chests and abdomens. Most of the sensory nerves of the trunk are distributed along the sides and the flanks. In animals that are more bipedal, the front of the body is much wider and capable of more sensory contacts. Even with such a broad surface area, apes generally only make brief contact with a small area around their genitals when engaged in sex. When human beings make love, however, many more sensory nerve endings are involved in producing the total experience.

In human sexual intercourse, the frontal position also offers the greatest amount of stimulation for the female clitoris by the male. The face-to-face position allows pressure from the male pubic area to be applied to the clitoral region of the female. Frontal lovemaking also puts the hands in nearly the best position for touching the entire body of the partner, in order to stimulate the sensitive skin and erogenous zones. With faces in close contact, the kiss, perhaps the most meaningful stimulus of sexual contact, can take place. The highly sensitive lips and the mucous membranes of the mouth can make contact with the lips and skin of the partner and this can continue on through lovemaking. In the kissing and touching around the face and neck, the erogenous areas of the nose, ears, and neck are continually aroused. Since neural activity in the body is electrical, the legion of body contacts and continuous erogenous stimulation in frontal lovemaking send powerful currents of electrical charge throughout the body. We speak of being "turned on" sexually without realizing how appropriate that metaphor really is.

The angle of the human female vagina also seems designed for frontal lovemaking. In dogs the vagina is relatively straight and receives the dog's penis easily as he mounts from the rear. If the human female positions herself on all fours, her vagina will not be at the best angle for intercourse. Bending her head and shoulders down to the bed will reposition her vagina for easier lovemaking.

Front-to-front sexual love is primarily a personal experience. It is face to face—an admission that something greater than just the momentary, mutual stimulation of each other's genitals is occurring. Our partner is a person, a name, with needs, desires, and hopes as real and as valuable as our own. It is personhood, imaged in the face, to which we learn to give, to surrender. It is good to be reminded in the middle of sexual pleasure that we are united with another in this life. Joys and pains are best when shared. The foundation of being a person and of being a lover is the act of knowing another and thus stretching beyond ourselves. Major sexual problems can arise from our inability to go beyond the few inches and few minutes of genital pleasure. To be centered on the other is the key to sexual satisfaction. It is a mystery. We must not focus entirely on self or the self's private pleasure, lest we lose everything. Looking at, touching, speaking to, and caring for the other person is the essence of sexual pleasure. Our bodies are designed to help us not miss this fact.

Frontal mating is not entirely absent in the animal world, but it is rare enough to be considered a near accident among primates who stumble on the anatomical possibility. Some frontal mating has been observed in gorillas, pygmy chimpanzees, and orangutans. Since these observations are such rare and generally isolated instances in captivity, they are not accurate portrayals of primate sexual activity. When primates occasionally mate in this way, only their genitals are in contact, as in the dorsal-ventral position. It is not similar to the whole-body experience of the human being. Some observers describe a "prolonged eye contact" between the primates when in this frontal position, but it is difficult to assess the importance of this. Rather than anthropomorphize something romantic in this eye contact, it seems reasonable to think that each of the two animals is surprised to see a face staring at it during the genital experience.

Explaining why human beings mate face to face is difficult for the naturalists who feel they must look for some advantageous evolutionary adaptation. Desmond Morris, in *The Naked Ape*, makes an attempt.[1] He wonders if nature provided the human female with large breasts to imitate the fleshy human buttocks. Nature's purpose was to attract the male around to the front to mate, thus to benefit from all the advantages that a personal relationship would have for survival. I do not think anyone really believes that this is a satisfactory or complete explanation.

Unique Sexual Bodies

The human female is the only female in the world who can have an orgasm. Does that sound important? Wherever there is a feature of our bodies that is totally unique, it must be important. The unique design of the body human always contributes to the personhood of the human being.

It is difficult for words to capture the meaning of the sexual experience for men and women, particularly the climactic, orgasmic phase. Male and female orgasms are physiologically quite similar. In both sexes intense sexual arousal results in genital vasocongestion and muscular tension, followed by irregular muscle spasms that quickly become rhythmic, lasting several seconds. The orgasm itself is accompanied by heavy breathing, pounding heart, skin flushing, and sweating. The intensity of the physical

1. Desmond Morris, *The Naked Ape* (New York: Dell Publishing Co., Inc., 1969).

pleasure associated with an orgasm is affected by the anticipation of climax, the intensity of arousal, the relationship with the partner, the act of sharing, fantasizing, and the sense of achievement. It cannot be adequately described or analyzed objectively. If we think we have words for it, we obviously do not understand it. There are two main differences between male and female orgasms. The first is the time in sexual arousal required to reach orgasm, usually several to ten minutes in the male and twice that in the female. The second difference is that men have an absolute refractory phase following their orgasm, during which time they cannot achieve another orgasm. Women can have multiple orgasms in rapid succession.

The female orgasm is a complicated response involving motor, neural, and physiological elements. Biologists would predict gradual approximations of this response in evolutionary history, but none are found. Desmond Morris speculates in *The Naked Ape* about the advantage of the female orgasm to the survival of the human species.[2] He feels that the orgasm serves the purpose of leaving the female exhausted and flat on her back for many minutes. Since she does not get up immediately after intercourse, the male seminal fluid is less likely to drain out of her vagina. Anything is possible, but surely Morris feels that nature could have thought of something more simple to assist conception.

The major organ of sensitivity important for the female orgasm is the clitoris. It is the erectile organ of the female that corresponds to the male penis and is located above and just outside the entrance to the vagina. The size of the clitoris seems to have little or no influence on the intensity of the female orgasm. The clitoris performs its function as

2. Ibid.

the center of arousal in the female pelvis because it contains as many nerve endings as the penis. Amazingly, the clitoris seems to be the only organ of any creature that has pleasure as its only purpose.

Female primates do have a clitoris as part of their sexual anatomy, but what exact function it has is not clear. Some South American monkeys have an elongated clitoris, which resembles a penis and makes it difficult to tell the sexes apart. This type of clitoris does not appear to be erectile. In some species the clitoris is small and hidden from view, while in others it is quite long and pendulous and may have a bone in its tip.

Some scientists have expended a lot of research effort to demonstrate that some female animals do experience orgasms. Female primate behaviors during the act of mating do include staccato grunting (in some baboons) and reaching back and clutching (rhesus monkeys). These behaviors have occurred simultaneously with the male's ejaculation. One experiment has reported physiological measures of orgasm in macaque monkeys.[3] Unfortunately, this study was performed on females mounting females in homosexual episodes. The dominant females mounted other females, performed a series of pelvic thrusts, and then showed the characteristic male ejaculatory-like response of a round-mouth face. The mounted female also showed responses typical of a female after a male has ejaculated. These results are certainly clouded by the fact that since only females were used in the sex act, there could not be any penile insertion or actual ejaculation. Perhaps the mounting female was able to create enough friction through pelvic thrusts to climax. It is also possible that the

3. D. A. Goldfoot, H. Westerborg-van Loon, W. Growneveld, and A. Koos Slob, "Behavioral and Physiological Evidence of Sexual Climax in the Female Stump-Tailed Macaque (*Macaca Arctoides*)," *Science*, 1980, *208*, 1477–79.

females were imitating male behaviors, including facial responses, in the absence of males and actual sexual intercourse. An EEG, a heart-rate monitor, and a uterine-contraction monitor were used, and these did show changes during the round-mouth–face periods of the mounting females. But these same changes in physiological responses can occur in the absence of orgasm, even in human women. The researchers also admitted that female monkeys in normal heterosexual mating also show the round-mouth responses, although not during any particular phase of the mating cycle. Whatever these results might mean, some things are clear. If anything resembling female orgasm exists in the animal world, it is an insignificant and exceedingly rare occurrence. A female orgasm in the animal world would seem also to serve no evolutionary purpose, since the females are motivated by cycles of heat and ovulation, and mating occurs reliably without the female climax. The extremely short duration of animal intercourse, measured in seconds rather than minutes, also argues against a successful orgasm in animal females.

The relatively small size of the penis in all male animals suggests that successfully achieving entrance to the vagina and releasing the seed is the goal of animal sexual intercourse. The human male has by far a larger penis than any primate. It is very long and thick, even when compared to that of the much larger gorilla. The size of the human penis guarantees much more stimulation of the female genitals. During intercourse the clitoral region of the female is pulled and pushed. Therefore, the orgasm of the human female due to this clitoral stimulation seems to be a product of the size of the human penis. If entry and ejaculation were the only goals of sexual intercourse, then the human penis is poorly designed because its size makes entry more difficult.

The flaccid human penis typically varies from seven to twelve centimeters in length. During erection the penile length will increase to seventeen to nineteen centimeters. Estimates of the size of the erect penis of the gorilla are less than seven centimeters. (These are obviously estimates because no one has had the courage to make an exact measurement.) The male chimpanzee has a slightly longer penis than the gorilla, but it is still very thin and pointed. It is longer because the swelling around the female chimpanzee's genitals during the first half of her menstrual cycle increases the length of her genital tract. Female gorillas have no such swelling. Orangutans and gibbons also have thin, pointed penises. Inside the penis of most primates, but not man, is a small bony skeleton called the baculum, which varies considerably in its relative size and contour. Located in the tip of the penis, the baculum probably serves to increase the stiffness of the small primate penis, which has less blood engorgement for stiffening.

The human penis is constructed of erectile tissue arranged in three longitudinal columns. Erectile tissue has a meshwork of cavernous spaces that are fed by capillaries and small arterioles and drained by small veins. When the arterioles supplying the blood spaces dilate, a tenfold increase of blood rushes in and is trapped. Since fluid is incompressible, the penis grows rigid. The engorged blood spaces block the thin veins that would let the blood out, and the erection is thus maintained.

Erectile tissue, which is also found in female genitals, breasts, and the human nose, functions as a marvelous contrivance for producing variable sensitivities in the human body. To merely design a body with extremely sensitive genitals for sexual pleasure would create problems during nonsexual activities. We would not want to have such sensitive genitals that we have an orgasm every time the wind blows on us. That would be inconvenient. The need is for genitals that are highly sensitive during love-making but relatively insensitive at other times. Erectile tissue fills this need. The erect penis or breast exposes much more of the sensitive skin to the stimulation of sexual activity. With the increased blood flow to the organ, neural activity becomes much more pronounced.

The human body possesses another area of sexual uniqueness. Solomon poetically calls it a mountain of spices, then compares its softness to deerskin. He is writing about the female breast. The human female is the only female creature with large spherical breasts. Other animals have nipples, not breasts. The breasts are part of the body human's sexual-response apparatus and are not primarily maternal milk glands. Breast growth commences at puberty as the chief secondary sex characteristic of the female. Further growth comes during pregnancy and nursing, when the breast becomes capable of milk production. All primates nurse their young quite adequately with just nipples. In fact, the breast of a human female is not the most efficient instrument for nursing the young. I recall watching our first child nurse. At times he seemed very frustrated with the whole process. He would nurse for a few seconds and then draw back and cry. Immediately he would grope for the nipple again, but the same problem repeated itself. This is called by some the "fighting the breast" response. It looks as if the baby cannot get comfortable or does not like what he is drinking. In actuality, the baby is having trouble breathing while nursing from the breast. Since the large breast often covers the baby's nose while he is sucking, he cannot breathe. Baby-bottle nipples have a much more efficient shape and size for sucking than a mother's breast. Primates, unlike human women, are flat-chested, but they have long nipples for efficient nursing.

The enlarged breast serves the purpose of an additional erogenous zone on the female body. It is a part of her form that attracts the male, and caressing it brings them both pleasure. Except for the face, there is no area of the body that gets more attention from both men and women in our culture than the breast. Unfortunately, we focus too much on the size of the breast and in that way prepare millions of women for disappointment because they feel they do not "measure up." What we need to realize is that it is not the breasts' size that is of importance, but that all breasts are extremely sensitive to touching and caressing. The absolute size of a breast does not change its sensitivity. Breasts were designed for the pleasure of women and men and serve to enrich the face-to-face love of two people.

Animal Sex

The body human is obviously designed for person-to-person sexual experiences, since it is made for face-to-face mating and the human female shares in sexual pleasure. Human sexual intercourse, therefore, can exist not only on the level of physical procreation, but also as a means of personal interaction. Sexual experiences in the animal world seem to be very shallow when compared to the rich possibilities of the human encounter.

Other animals are locked into cycles of heat and ovulation, and their sexual lives fit into the fabric of nature. An animal's sexual activity is strongly controlled by the ovulatory cycle of the female. In the human female, peak sexual arousal and ovulation do not coincide, and sexual arousal can occur at any time, for both male and female. Nor are we restricted to limited seasonal breeding periods as in most lower animals. Human sexual activity is much more intense and personal, usually occurring in some sort of pair-bonded state. Few monkeys develop prolonged pair-bond relationships. If any behavior patterns exist before mating in monkeys and apes, they are brief facial expressions or simple vocalizations. The act of copulation in the animal world is usually brief, and this brevity ensures safety from predators. Their copulatory act serves only to plant the seed. Baboon intercourse, for example, takes no longer than seven or eight seconds. The male mounts, has ten to fifteen pelvic thrusts, ejaculates, and then both male and female go on with life as usual.

Man is truly the most sexually active of all creatures. In the majority of animal species, the female is receptive to the male only at certain short times of the year. The changes in the female that make her receptive to the male are referred to as "heat" by animal breeders and "estrus" by physiologists. Some animals, such as the dog, are monestrous and have a single estrus period each mating season. The cow, mouse, and rat have a series of estrus cycles during each mating season and therefore are called polyestrous. Many monkeys in the wild breed only during a single season. In captivity or in controlled environments of the laboratory, monkeys will often breed year-round because their hormones are no longer being influenced by the environmental factors of a wild habitat, such as day length, humidity, and diet. These monkeys normally copulate only during a few months a year, thus ensuring that the young will be born when they are most likely to survive.

The female langur is a good example of the restraints on primate sexual activity. She is not sexually receptive for much of her life—not when she is pregnant (about one-fourth of her adult life), and not when nursing or weaning her young (about one-half of her adult life). In the brief periods between pregnancies, she is sexually active for only less than a week each month. All of this reduces her to periods of sexual activity comprising only 1 to 3 percent of her adult life.

The control of hormones over primate mating patterns is illustrated by the baboons. The dominant male baboons will mate with a female only when she is at the height of estrus. As the estrus of the female increases, the skin around her genitals swells up with water until it is several inches thick. It is only then that the dominant males are ready to mate with her, thus assuring mating while she is ovulating and most likely to conceive.

Rodents that live in open spaces and are not safe from predators have a single ejaculation during a very brief mount. Those species that are safer from predators in burrows or trees may have locking copulations in which the penis remains in the vagina for long periods of time, apparently to ensure that seminal fluid will not spill out. Cats and rabbits ovulate only after they mate, a condition known as reflex ovulation or coitus-induced ovulation.

When a male animal is exhausted after several copulations, he will generally have renewed interest and vigor if a new female is presented to him. This is especially true of the ram. In one experiment a ram copulated with twelve different females before the experimenters got tired of shifting sheep around. Some experimenters even tried to fool the rams by putting coats and Halloween masks on the same female.[4] That had to look ridiculous! But the males were never fooled. They apparently can sense the same ewe. This phenomenon, very common in animals, guarantees that all the available females have a chance to become

4. Neil R. Carlson, *Physiology of Behavior*, 2nd ed. (Boston: Allyn and Bacon, Inc., 1980) p. 331.

pregnant. This also works against monogamy in most animals. Birds are notable exceptions to animal polygamy, since one male and female form a breeding pair for a season or for a lifetime. Lifelong monogamy has been found in doves, for example, and their constancy has made them the symbol of love.

The mating of primates, particularly in the apes, is vastly different from that of human beings and is strongly tied to internal physiology and the environment. Male orangutans are very assertive sexually. More than one researcher has used the term *rape* to describe their style, both in captivity and in the wild. The male orangutan will mate at any time during the menstrual cycle, but if a situation occurs when a female can decide when to mate, then variations in her interest become apparent. Unlike gorillas and chimpanzees, orangutans in the wild will associate with females only for sexual reasons. When a young lady has trouble with the persistent sexual advances of her date, she makes a mistake to call him a "gorilla," when "orangutan" would be a much more appropriate label.

The female gorilla has a three-day estrus during the middle of her menstrual cycle. Before the estrus her odor begins to change and the males sniff at her genitals and armpits. During estrus she seems attracted to the male, and to get his attention she frequently stares at him with pursed lips and stands stiff-legged. The female usually invites copulation by showing her genitals to the male as she backs up to him. The male will then mount in the dorsal-ventral position for a brief time of about thirty-six pelvic thrusts before he ejaculates. Both animals make cooing sounds during copulation, with the female occasionally screaming. The gorillas confine their mating to this one-to-four–day period during the middle of the menstrual cycle;

thus they seem more controlled by their gonadal hormone than any other ape.

Nature's control over gorilla sexual behavior is partially seen in how early sexual behaviors show up in gorilla development. At from one and a half to two and a half years, baby gorillas play at copulation. Young baby males mount baby females and even mount mature females and show thrusting behavior. This is also seen in macaques and baboons. This early mating-like activity is not expressed with full intensity or completeness until puberty.

In chimpanzees, the female may initiate copulation by presenting her genitals to the male and backing up toward him in a crouched posture. She looks back at him as she does so. The female will always present to the male in response to his courtship display, which includes bipedal swaggering, glaring, leaping, and beckoning. While either partner may initiate copulation, both in the wild and in captivity, the male chimpanzee is sexually more assertive than the female. (In gorillas, the male only rarely invites copulation.)

Chimpanzees copulate in the dorsal-ventral position, with ejaculation occurring after five to ten seconds. During copulation the male pants loudly while the female looks back at him with a "grinning" expression and makes squeaking sounds. Chimpanzees occasionally form short partnerships, but generally any male can mate with any female. Copulation may occur at any time during the female's thirty-five–day menstrual cycle, but it more generally takes place as her sexual skin swells and turns pink than when it is declining. Ovarian hormones seem very important in controlling the mating behavior of chimpanzees, since research has shown that after females are ovariectomized, mating frequencies decrease markedly.

Jane van Lawick-Goodall describes a typical period of
estrus for a dominant, older female named Flo.[5] First, Flo
presented her pink posterior to Goliath, and he mated
with her in the typical nonchalant manner of the chimpanzee. He was squatting, almost sitting in an upright position, one hand full of fruit because he had been eating.
Goliath, similar to all chimpanzees, had the briefest possible intercourse, lasting for only ten to fifteen seconds. A
few minutes later, Flo was approached by another chimpanzee, David Graybeard. He sat on the ground, shook a
twig at Flo, all the while staring intently at her. She immediately ran over to him and backed into him. Next, Evered
gave the typical courtship posture and Flo obliged at once,
as she had for the others. The next day Flo copulated with
all the males in the area, ten or more. It was the same all
week long. Wherever she went she was followed by a
whole troop of males. She could not sit or lie down or move
slightly without all male eyes watching her every move.
When she rose to move on, every male instantly did likewise. Whenever during the day there was anything exciting going on, such as leaving their nests in the morning or
arriving at a new food source, all the males mated with Flo,
each in turn. No one fought over her. Each simply had his
turn. Flo's estrus was especially long, three weeks as opposed to the usual ten days, and each day continued like
the day before it, totally exhausting Flo. During the extra-
long mating period Flo seemed to form a strong attachment to a particular male, but he did not protest other
males' mating with her, which is typical of chimpanzees.
Finally, Flo's posterior shrank down to its former size, and
all the males immediately left her alone. Flo did not "go
pink" again for five years. Younger females usually go into

    5. Jane van Lawick-Goodall, *In the Shadow of Man* (Boston: Houghton Mif-
flin Co., 1971) pp. 82–83.

estrus again after their young chimpanzee is about four-teen months old, but older females like Flo do not go into estrus for four or five years. As a result of this particular estrus cycle, Flo conceived and bore a male. (The chimpanzees' sex life sounds like promiscuity unleashed, but for some reason it does not sound too exciting.)

The biological strings pulling their sexual behaviors are seen early in the life of chimpanzees. Young male chimpanzees show a very precocious sexual development. From an early age, all the males show an intense interest in the pink swellings of the female. Chimpanzee infants frequently attempt to mount females when they sit down. When a pink female is in the group, "play" for the young male infants seems to be running up to her, mounting her, and engaging in mock pelvic thrusting.

Personalized Human Sexuality

There is almost no basis for comparing human sexual behavior with that of the animal world in general. Our bodies were designed for sex as if people mattered. If we refuse to follow this design written in our bodies, then our sex lives will suffer. The bulk of human sexual behavior is personal to some degree. We are highly unique in the animal world with our lengthy (even years) of pre-copulatory activities. Our dating and courtship periods are extremely long by animal standards. The bulk of our contact with the opposite sex, both before and after marriage, is not through sexual intercourse but through conversation and simple body contact. Even prior to sexual intercourse itself, the human preoccupation with romance and love seems important. Intense personal feelings are generated with candlelight dinners, music, playful games, and simple shared pleasures. Foreplay to human sexual intercourse may last several minutes or even several hours. The look, the caress, and the kiss are intended for pleasure and to lead the other to pleasure. After intercourse, kissing and touching and conversation continue. This is hardly like the fifteen-second chimpanzee stampede.

The human male and female are sexually receptive at any time, year-round. Even the pregnant or nursing female is sexually receptive to the male. In spite of our sexual problems and perversions, we are still the sexiest creatures alive. In spite of all of our prostitution, masturbation, and casual promiscuity, human sex is still bonded to human love and affection. In spite of our divorces, we are still militantly monogamous. Although human beings frequently depart from the optimum of a personal sexual relationship, this is no reason to identify human with animal sexuality. The unique thing about human beings is that they are capable of personal sex, even if they do not act that way some of the time.

Unlike animals, our thoughts and imaginations play a major role in our sexual arousal. The human mind captures the essence of love and purpose and giving. The mind is attracted to warmth, passion, humor, honesty, kindness, face, and form. We are designed to be aroused and satisfied by people, not by leather sheets.

It is clear from studying the human body that pleasure in sex is important for both partners. This is particularly true in the female, whose breasts are a unique erogenous zone and who can experience an orgasm. Mutual pleasure and personal sharing are important. What is interesting about the potential for an orgasm in both partners is the well-known fact that it takes human females longer to reach a sexual climax than males. At first glance the design of such a pleasure system seems flawed. In fact, in our own married lives, it may have perplexed us why the sexes differ in this way. The design is not flawed. Having different speeds to arousal and climax puts the human male and female in a position of needing to communicate. We have to talk about what is pleasurable. The male has to slow down, partially ignore the fire in his own loins, and consider the other person in his life. Rather than frustrating them, this design actually increases the potential physical enjoyment of each partner. Instead of deadening our senses and thinking about nonsense in order to avoid too early a climax, we are designed and encouraged and commanded to think of another, to give to another.

Pleasure in sex depends on more than activity in localized erogenous zones. There are no specialized pleasure receptors in the skin. Sexual pleasure is related to, but more than, rhythmic contractions and neural impulses. Our total experience of both pleasure and pain depends on our anticipation of them and the importance and meaning attached to them. It is impossible to know exactly what an animal feels during its sex act, but animal experiences in general must be greatly limited by the animal's cognitive faculties. The localized genital experience of an ape may not produce an experience of intense pleasure, at least as we know it, but something more similar to a release of tension. Similarly, when we are so hungry that we rapidly eat an entire pizza, what pleasure do we remember deriving from it? We could not resist eating the pizza, and we caught a brief experience of pleasure, but the activity of eating was driven and automatic.

When male chimpanzees mate, they are very often attacked by immature chimpanzees in the group. As soon as the young chimpanzees observe a mature male and female mating, they rush up to the couple and try to interfere. They jump all over the male, pulling at him and screaming. Males are never so tolerant of young chimpanzees as they are during these times. The male may be almost lost to view as half a dozen baby chimps crowd over him, clinging to his head and face. The adult male simply turns away and ignores their interruption and gets on with what he is doing. Why the infants behave that way we do not know.

Imagine if our sex lives fit the following scenario. A male chimpanzee has just started eating some bananas when a female "in pink" backs up to him. He does not know why, but he feels a force compelling him to mate. He drops low to the ground but does not drop his bananas. Although he feels frustrated at not finishing his bananas, he feels driven to mate. He begins to mate, only half aware of what he is doing. Six juveniles suddenly descend upon him, screaming and punching. In twelve seconds it is all over and fades rapidly from his memory. The chimp resumes eating his bananas.

By human standards, chimpanzee sex experiences may be limited, but they probably represent the height of sexual experience in the animal world. Consider the angler fish. The deep-sea angler has her own fishing rod growing out of the top of her head and hanging in front of her mouth. The tip of the rod shines and acts as bait. Hungry fish attack the bait and are caught by the angler. The female angler may grow to be three feet long, but the male is only three inches long. Soon after birth the male angler finds a female and fastens onto her side with his mouth. Their skin grows together and they are never parted. The male has become a type of subcutaneous sperm bank. That sounds like an unusual and even exciting sex life, but not exactly the "two become one flesh" of the Genesis accounts.

It is interesting that Jane Goodall was married during her field work with chimpanzees. She must have reflected on her own sexual experience compared with those of the chimpanzees, when she wrote about the chimpanzee relationships:

> . . . . although such relationships may be shadowy forerun-
> ners of human love affairs, I cannot conceive of chimpan-
> zees developing emotions, one for the other, comparable in
> any way to the tenderness, the protectiveness, tolerance,
> and spiritual exhilaration that are the hallmarks of human
> love in its truest and deepest sense. Chimpanzees usually
> show a lack of consideration for each other's feelings
> which in some ways may represent the deepest gulf be-
> tween them and us. For the male and female chimpanzee
> there can be no exquisite awareness of each other's body—
> let alone each other's mind. The most a female can expect
> of her suitor is a brief courtship display, a sexual contact
> lasting at most half a minute, and sometimes a session of
> social grooming afterward. Not for them the romance, the
> mystery, the boundless joys of human love.[6]

It is interesting that no female of any animal species in the world has a hymen (the maidenhead), except the human female. It almost seems as if the body human is saying that the first sexual encounter for a woman is not to be entered into lightly. Something personal and hallowed is at stake.

6. Ibid., p. 194.

4 The Long Childhood

Man is the only creature who refuses to grow up.

There is something of the weed in every child. Persistent and hearty, little weeds survive in every garden, no matter how much we stomp on or mutilate them. The frail-looking weed, for some reason, manages to pop up through the cement of older streets and sidewalks. It does not appear that the weed is all-powerful so much as all the power of nature is funneling through the weed. Weeds may not appear outwardly strong, but they are the dominant life form in my garden. So, too, the human child is the weakest of creatures but, as a mature person, becomes the dominant life form on earth.

Short of locking up a child in a coal cellar for several years, there is very little that the human environment can do to stop the emergence of personhood in the child. The little baby will grow mentally, culturally, and socially into full humanness, with the assistance of several physical attributes that are unique to the body human. The erect posture of the child frees its hands to do what its mind imagines. The brain of the child contains complicated neural programming for later language and thinking skills. But the most unexpected physical advantage to the human infant in its growth toward personhood is that it is physically much weaker than other young animals and is extremely slow to develop to maturity. Complete physical and social maturity comes so late for the child that it seems that man is the only creature who refuses to grow up.

The Long and Weak Childhood

The human being has the longest maturation span of any creature. Nature's animals are much more prepared for physical survival, even at birth, than are humans. The newborn wildebeest stands and runs off with its mother five minutes after birth. The baby elephant will follow its mother all day long within twenty-four hours after birth. The newborn human is, on the other hand, a completely helpless creature. The neonate's sole physical preparation for survival seems to be the reflex to suck. Even newborn primates, who are comparatively weak at birth for animals, will cling to their mothers shortly after birth with a tenacious strength, leaving the mother free to roam on all fours. The human infant has a grasping reflex, but—unlike primates—its musculature is poorly developed at birth. Since the human baby cannot hold on to the parent, it must be carried everywhere.

The human baby begins life with absolute dependency on others, rather than being born physically ready to compete for life. The human baby also grows very slowly and does not come close to its mature size for many years. The child likewise enters puberty at a much later time than animals, giving it an extended childhood. The human infant is strange, indeed, when it is compared to the majority of the animals of the world, which are up and moving around a few hours after birth, or a month at most. Carnivores and prosimians reach statural maturity, on the average, by three years. Apes, with the slowest maturation rate of all mammals, are mature by eight or nine years. What is the human infant capable of at one day old? one month old? three years? nine years? What advantage is gained by such an incredible prolongation of human weakness and delay of maturity?

We humans are 5 percent of our adult size at birth. By fourteen years we will be 60 percent of our mature stature. But not until we are about twenty will we have 90 to 95 percent of our eventual size. Finally, in our middle thirties, we reach our peak size and strength. Most animals are, on the average, 60 percent of their full size at one year and 90 to 95 percent of their maximal size at three.

The newborn baby has 350 bones in its body, which must gradually fuse together into the 206 bones of the adult human's body. (The three inner ear bones do not grow because they are full-sized at birth.) The bones of the cranium of the newborn child are not completely joined together, leaving large openings in the skull that have yet to be ossified. The soft spot at the top of a new baby's skull is one of these. This loose structure of bones in the skull allows the head of the fetus to change shape in order to fit through the birth canal. Many new parents have worried about the distortion of their newborn's head, not realizing it was only temporary. By age two, most of the large holes of the baby's skull have closed, but ossification of the human skull is not complete until age nineteen. This delayed bone ossification is essential in order that the brain case remain relatively pliable for the continued brain growth so important in humans.

Most of a baby's bones are not fully formed at birth. Many are still soft, clear cartilage. For example, a newborn has no finished wrist bones. Even by the age of two there are only two finished bones in each wrist. There are five in the five-year-old. Finally, by age twelve, all eight wrist bones have formed into hard, white, flexible bones. Unlike animals, the young human is not capable of using its most important limbs with strength and flexibility. A very young child cannot easily wield a hammer with strength and accuracy because of the wrist's retarded development. The human child is clearly not prepared for physical survival as are primates, who will have been playing Tarzan from an early age. It is interesting that the hand, which plays such an important role in the expression of our humanness, takes so long to develop to mature use. The child begins with wrist and hand bones that are only bits of cartilage. In regular steps, the cartilage hardens into bone. The process is so predictable that we can tell the age of a child's skeleton by comparing the wrist to established averages. The speed of a child's skeletal growth can also be tracked by regular X-rays of the hand and wrist.

The baby's pelvis is also made up of several smaller bones that will grow together with age. The ilium, the ischium, and the pubis are joined by cartilage early in life. At approximately age twelve a hardening and joining begins, which is not complete until age twenty to twenty-five. The bones of the arms and legs are also not unified and solid for a time. Each arm- or leg-bone shaft is separated from the expanded ends. With the growth of the child, the shafts grow and unite with the ends to form a solid bone.

Growth in the infant is therefore abnormally extended over many years. Life begins at about seven pounds for the helpless human. There is relatively rapid growth for two years, and then growth slows slightly until age six, when it slows down to a gradual pace until puberty. More rapid growth for boys is seen from eleven to seventeen years and in girls from ten to fifteen. Most of body growth is then completed by nineteen in girls and twenty-five in boys.

The onset of puberty begins in girls as early as age ten, and 80 percent have menstruated by fourteen years. Pubic hair, breast enlargement, and a broadening of the hips begin at puberty. In boys, puberty begins at about age eleven. By fourteen, 80 percent of boys have entered puberty. Pubic and facial hair, a deeper voice, and a widening of the shoulders appear at this time. In both sexes, the genital organs also accelerate their growth.

The process of myelination (the growth of insulating material around neurons) is not complete at birth in humans. Therefore, various body behaviors cannot develop until corresponding nerves are myelinated. Good vision has only a short wait for myelination of the optic tract. However, the nerves connected to the muscles of the legs are not fully myelinated until the baby is more than a year old, and the complex interplay of muscles involved in walking is delayed that long.

The slow growth of human infants and their poorly developed muscles and unmyelinated nerves guarantee that babies can make only trivial movements at birth. At one month, for example, a baby girl begins to raise her head above the ground when lying on her stomach. At two months she can raise her chest off the ground with her arms. At three months the baby can reach toward objects. At four months she is just beginning to be able to sit up with support. At five months the infant can hold objects in her hands. At six months she is sitting in a high chair and more easily grasping objects. At seven months she crawls and can sit without assistance for those family pictures. At nine months she may be able to stand by holding on to furniture and is crawling rapidly. Walking may be seen as early as nine months or as late as fifteen months. In this time period she is also learning to crawl upstairs. All of these are, of course, average ages for development of motor and locomotion skills in the child. This developmental progression illustrates the slow growth and maturation of the child in areas of physical strength.

The maturation rates for animals show considerable variability, but, in general, the growth rates are very rapid when compared to that of the human being. Rapid growth rates would be in harmony with the survival needs of the wild. With rapid growth the young animals are quickly able to fend for themselves, and the mother can easily raise more young. Primates have slower maturity rates than most animals because they have higher learning capabilities, and a slightly longer childhood gives them more time for learning. Smaller prosimians, such as the mouse lemur, are sexually mature at one year old. This may be compared to the average monkey, whose infant dependency ends at age one and is sexually mature at about three and a half years. The gorilla's infancy-dependency period ends by three, and sexual maturity arrives at about six or seven. By contrast, human children leave behind their infant dependency by eight and have usually reached sexual maturity by fourteen. Social maturity, measured by near-maximum physical growth and well-established dominance patterns, is reached by about seven years in the average monkey, ten in the gorilla, and eighteen in man. Humans clearly mature more slowly than even these slow-developing primates.

Rhesus-monkey infants are able to raise their chests and heads by pushing up on their elbows twenty-four to forty-eight hours after birth. The human infant must wait one or two months for the same ability. Baby baboons will walk when they are one week old, even though their mother carries them most of the time. Baby baboons are also able to touch nearly any object within their reach at four weeks, which shows good eye-hand coordination. Humans need five months for the same ability to develop.

Newborn gorillas are very helpless at birth. Yet, although they cannot focus their gaze or localize sounds, they possess a number of behavioral reflexes important for survival. They possess the rooting reflex (head movements that search for the mother's breast) and the sucking reflex. Baby gorillas also have very strong grasping and suspension reflexes (for grasping with hands and feet and hanging with no support). Human neonates also have hand-grasp and suspension reflexes, but they are considerably weaker and the reflexes disappear within three weeks. In the gorilla they continue for three months and merge into strong voluntary movements. With this strength the baby gorilla can cling tightly to its mother as she moves about.

Chimpanzees have the same superior physical capabilities as infant gorillas. But young chimpanzees seem to be more emotionally attached to their mothers and continue to depend on them almost to puberty. Most chimpanzee youngsters continue to suckle and sleep with their mothers for over four years, and they are six before they move around a lot without their mothers. Females reach puberty at about seven years, although they will not menstruate or be attractive to males for another year or two. Males reach puberty at seven or eight years but will not reach full size for several more years.

Rapid Personal Growth

The human child may be weak and relatively helpless for years, but this seems to be only in the physical realm. Whereas physical strengths and abilities show up relatively late, social, personal, and cognitive skills develop extremely early, particularly in the first two years of life. The explosion of language at age two is a good example. At two, since the child has just recently learned to walk and possesses only a fraction of its peak physical size and strength, he or she is not prepared for independent survival. Yet, the young human develops the ultimate personal skill almost overnight between two and three years of age. Language does not actually aid the child's physical survival, since his parents have already learned to respond to his every need. Nor is this speaking two-year-old likely to be a contributor to the learning and culture of the world for several more decades. It is highly striking that the child's body propels him into language so early, while his physical development is so unusually detained. It is not really surprising, though, if we accept the notion that personal growth is more important for the child than physical growth, that the body human is designed to give the child maximal personal interaction early in life.

A newborn infant may be a helpless creature, totally dependent on the parents' care, but it is not passive and simply waiting for adult contact and care. Very quickly the infant develops abilities that actively put it into interaction with others in its environment. We have already seen that, while it may not be an innate response, the child by two months of age has a decided preference for looking at faces, especially the eyes. This behavior facilitates frequent eye-to-eye contact with the parents. When the baby's glance to parents is combined with a hearty smile, an invaluable interaction between parent and child occurs. If a parent does not respond when the infant makes eye contact, the baby shows signs of distress and begins to lessen visual interaction with that person.

The newborn has even more astonishing abilities to relate to people. At one week old the infant recognizes its mother's voice and can pick it out of a group of female voices. This ability is apparently begun as the infant resides in the womb, ever hearing Mother's voice. At two weeks the infant can recognize that its mother's face and voice belong together as a unit. Babies pay special attention to their fathers' voices as well. At several weeks old an infant begins to show an entirely different attitude toward its father than its mother. Because of Dad's usually more vigorous, playful approach, the child is much more wide-eyed and excited around him. Close contact immediately after birth between the mother and infant, and probably the father and infant also, is extremely beneficial to mother and child. It is related to less infant crying, more rapid infant growth, increased affection and more self-confidence in the mother, and fewer instances of later child abuse. During their first hour alive, infants may spend 85 percent of the time in an awake, alert, inquisitive state.

Human children, like young chimpanzees and other apes, are inordinately curious. They are fascinated by new things. Everything becomes a toy to lift, to drop, to bang, to take apart, to invent new games with. This curiosity serves to bring the young into active contact with the world and counteract some of their fears. Baby chimpanzees actually appear to show more curiosity than baby humans because of their superior physical skills. They are able to explore, hold, and climb at an earlier age. But, after the first year, the chimpanzee begins to lose ground to the human, because its brain is not complex enough to expand on this curious bent, nor are its powers of concentration keen enough. Chimpanzees also lack the ability to share their discoveries or learn from others. The adult chimpanzee loses much of its explorative interest in the world, unlike the human being, who initiates rich encounters with other people and things all through life, personally, scientifically, and artistically.

The Speaking Child

The most amazing tool of the maturing child in its personal growth and interaction with the world is its use of language. The ability of a child to use language involves a heavy component of complex innate factors plus contact with a speaking environment. There are no transitional languages in the animal world to explain this amazing human ability, which appears highly developed by the time a child is three. Speech involves the use of an almost infinitely varied and modulated series of vocal sounds that depend upon a neurological complexity, a highly developed laryngeal apparatus, and a coordinated use of jaws, lips, and tongue. While animals may possess many gestures and vocalizations to communicate, only in man does the mind seem capable of conveying abstract ideas, relating the present to the past and the future, and conceiving of complex thoughts and feelings. All of this complexity begins at about age two. At this early age the child begins to share in the experiences of the group through the use of language. The world of experience is suddenly broadened, without the child having to experience everything directly. Verbal symbols are entry points into other people's thoughts and feelings, roads to worlds never visited, and part of the imaginative clay for unexplored possibilities and situations. For the young human, language is a powerful cultural force, helping to integrate the child into the cultural group. Language qualifies the child for the inheritance of custom and tradition, man's sociological genetics.

Shortly after the age of two, the average child can speak

nearly 300 words. By three, he or she may have tripled this. By four, most children have command of over 1,600 words, and they seem to use all of them every day with great repetition. By five years, the child knows over two thousand words. There is nothing even remotely approaching this ability in the animal world, including the language-conditioning experiments with chimpanzees. Certain birds may possess unusual powers of imitation, as is seen in the parrot, mynah bird, or crow. But with limited brains, those tongues have nothing to say.

The body human enables the child to personally enter the world of adults at an amazingly early age, though the body itself is not prepared to participate as a physical equal for almost two decades. The child's brain is complex enough to store all of the assumptions and memories and deductions that give him something to tell others. Anyone with children knows that the telling never stops (nor does the asking). Most animals can and probably do communicate feelings of pain, danger, anger, and sexual arousal, since these and other simple thoughts and feelings require only a modest armory of different sounds or signals. But the young child can experience a wonder about the nature of the universe and life—why an insect stops moving after it is stepped on; why crackers float in milk, but marbles do not; questions about family, death, right and wrong, or losing at a game. The child and the adult merge in philosophical conversation. "Philosophy" is not just the required metaphysics or epistemology classes in college; it is also a disarming conversation with a child. We may speculate on whether such abstractions can dimly glimmer in the mind of the ape, but it is clear that only the body human's brain and larynx are capable of producing the subtle, complex sounds of a mind at work.

The child's brain seems to be genetically prewired to acquire a complex system of language if he is exposed to any given speech community. Since there are no simple human languages anywhere in the world, scientists are continually amazed at the child's ability to acquire the highly complex, abstract, rule-governed knowledge involved in speaking. The evidence seems overwhelming that there are innate abilities in the body human that propel the child into language usage. These evidences include the ease with which a child learns language. We should think back to high school or college, when we were learning a second language. It was not easy. A two-year-old living in a foreign-language community would master the language by age three without any effort. Meanwhile, older students sweat pints of blood over simple daily quizzes. The innate connection in language is also seen in the fact that all children, not just a gifted few, acquire language with a skill not related to intelligence. In addition, the mouth-and-throat mechanical skills required to vocalize language are ready to match the child's desire to speak, even though the child's other mechanical skills are lagging far behind. Therefore, a child of three can talk a mile a minute, but he might seemingly die an early death trying to put his socks on.

Rather than view the child as a passive receiver of language skills resulting from the interaction of innate brain processes with a linguistic world, it seems as if the child's entry into language is an active encounter in dialogue, primarily with the mother. The child does not learn language by simply hearing it as the brain's language-acquisition device learns it. The child, out of necessity, begins with nonverbal communication with its mother and moves on to simple words. Both mother and child work hard to interpret the meaning and intent of communication attempts of the child. The mother may reduce the conversation to "baby talk" to provide reasonable conversation for the child to work with.

The Purpose of Childhood

Childhood offers no basic physical-survival benefits but instead provides opportunities for personal, social, mental, and moral development. To be a human being is more than physical survival, and the body human has been so designed. During the long childhood period, the child is physically dependent on others and therefore must interact with people. The baby's physical weakness guarantees that he or she will be almost constantly held and handled, aiding the development of the brain and later personal-social abilities.

The long childhood is designed for the growing, pliable human brain and its receptivity to the massive amount of material that a child must learn as a human being. The ape brain, pliable for a few years, very quickly seems to harden against new learning, but its need for learning also diminishes with maturity. Not one aspect of the baby's culture—tribal organization, language, religion, or artistic and scientific heritage—is carried in the germ cells. All of this must be passed from parent to child, from one generation to the next and primarily during the long and very formative childhood. The higher monkeys and the apes are able to learn in this way also, but such a long childhood is not needed, since there is so much less to pass on.

Because of the young human's physical dependency and the massive amount of culture and knowledge that must be transmitted to the child, the structure of family life is extremely important. The importance of the mother in the home may be seen in an unusual feature of the female human body. The fertility of the female will cease about twenty years before the end of her life. This passage of life is called menopause and has not been observed in apes.[1] A female ape could bear an infant while in an advanced state of senility. This twenty-year (or more) childless period for the human female is apparently designed to ensure that the mother can raise her last child to maturity.

The long maturation span of the body human guarantees that the young are an ever-present feature of the family. Since more children are born before the others mature, it makes the human parent's role the most difficult parenting responsibility in the animal world. It also staggers the development of children and exposes them to a variety of ages of brothers and sisters. This aids the beginning of socialization in the child, and the older children can learn the principles of responsibility and sharing. Older children can take part in the care and feeding of younger siblings and thus develop their own skills for future parental responsibilities. Even in chimpanzees, where adolescent females hover around mother chimp and the newborn, there is not the same family structure to continue the nurturing and training of older animals. Most animals "leave the nest" or mature and start their own families before another litter or infant is born.

The human father is also unique in comparison with the animal world in that he shares equally in the discipline, protection, feeding, and education of the young. Even though we fathers should perform much better at this role, it must be recognized what an exception father-parenting is in the animal world. Human children have special needs, and the family child-rearing responsibilities are great enough to require the active presence of the father in the home. Primate males do not take part in the responsi-

1. A. F. Dixson, *The Natural History of the Gorilla* (London: Weidenfeld and Nicolson, 1981) p. 158.

bilities of infant care and feeding. At best, they may share a friendly curiosity or playful attitude with the young. The male in many animal species is very antisocial and separates on his own or is excluded from the young animals by the females. The father, whoever he is, plays no role whatsoever in the chimpanzee family, and his presence is not needed for the social and physical development of the young. The human father, on the other hand, is not only an important provider for and protector of the young, but his presence and interaction with the children also seems of prime importance in the social and sexual development of both sons and daughters.

Feral Children

The total absence of human parents in the developmental life of a child is tragic and disastrous for the child. The importance of an early personal environment for young humans is shown rather dramatically by the case of feral children (those raised by animals). While being so raised, the basic physical needs of the child are generally met; but, with no human contact, the child does not develop into a person. Feral children seemed almost common in past years in India, where animals were not killed because of religious reservations, and in war and natural disaster areas, where children are commonly lost. Documentation exists on over thirty cases of feral children who were raised by wolves, bears, tigers, leopards, goats, sheep, and pigs.[2]

In all such cases of feral children, the lesson is clear. Children need human contacts and language in the early years of development in order to develop as whole per-

2. J. A. L. Singh and Robert M. Zingg, *Wolf-children and Feral Man* (New York: Harper and Brothers Publishers, 1939).

sons. Whenever a child had been raised from infancy by animals and not recovered until seven or eight years old, the child did not later adjust to society or learn a language. Whatever potential for humanness was latent, it utterly failed to develop during the critical early years of childhood. If this is universally true, it raises an interesting question of how human personality and culture ever developed in the first place. Since it takes human contact to develop humanness in a child, how did humanness first get its start?

The best-documented study of feral children is probably the case of the wolf girls of India. In parts of India in the early 1900s, young infants, especially girls, were left in the forests to die. Apparently, animals occasionally adopted these babies and, if guided more by a maternal instinct than a desire for food, raised them. Two such children were captured by the Reverend Singh on October 17, 1920. The two girls lived with a family of wolves in a huge termite mound. One appeared to be about eight years old, the other about a year and a half. Both girls were naked and covered with dirt, and their heads were covered with matted hair. They moved rapidly on all fours (hands and feet) and were quite difficult to chase and capture. Their only interests seemed to be raw meat and milk. The facial features of these little girls differed from other children, most likely because of diet. The ends of their jawbones projected out, probably from gnawing on bones. Their teeth were sharp and included longer canines than most humans. The insides of their mouths were blood-red. They were unable to stand or walk erect. Their eyes shone at night with an eerie glow from reflected light. This last observation is a rarity, but apparently can occur in human beings whose retina and choroid coat reflect light. The two little wolf girls, Kamala and Amala, had a good sense of smell and they ate like dogs, never using their hands, even to pick up food. They were ferocious with tooth and nail. These girls never seemed hot or cold and wore no clothes, even in the winter. They never shivered or perspired. If some of these attributes seem odd for a human being, we must remember that since there is some pliability in human development, the body develops in ways that reflect its use.

The two girls never laughed, and Kamala shed tears only once, when the younger girl, Amala, died of disease about a year after her capture. They both enjoyed the caressing affection of Mrs. Singh. Neither girl spoke, although the younger said, "Bhoo, bhoo" when she was thirsty. Both howled at night, however.

Kamala died on March 14, 1929, when she was almost seventeen. She had made more recovery than any other feral child who was recovered as late as eight years old. Kamala slowly began to develop more human qualities, as if they lay dormant within her. She began to cry more, fear dogs, sleep inside, and use the bathroom. She eventually learned fifty words and could use them in short sentences.

Other cases of feral children, which are less well documented by Singh and Zingg, include children lost in the forests and surviving unaided to maturity.[3] The Wild Boy of Avegron, the most famous of these children, appeared in 1799 at about seventeen years old. He gave no evidence of nurture by animals and could walk, run, and climb well. Although he gradually lost his bestial appearance, he seemed very retarded. He learned only three words before he died at forty years old.

In another case, in 1843, a three-year-old boy was grabbed by wolves and carried off. His parents were in the

3. Ibid.

field at the time but could not catch the wolves. The boy was recovered six years later, and his mother recognized his scars. She tried to raise him, but he showed no affection for her. He was released to live on the common charity of the village and apparently lived out his days as one of the village dogs.

One boy, Clemens of Overdyke, Germany, had been shut up as a very young child to live with pigs. He ate their food and associated entirely with the swine. When rescued, his intelligence was low and he never lost his affection for pigs. He did, though, laugh and talk some.

Many other feral cases are recorded by Singh and Zingg. In all instances, the children resembled in eating and locomotion the animal that had raised them. Very few of such children ever recovered any significant human functions.

A famous child of cruel isolation with problems similar to those of feral children was Kaspar Hauser of Germany.[4] He made a good recovery, but his was a strange type of isolation. Apparently the boy was heir to the throne of some petty German state and at his birth was sent away to be raised in isolation and to be released when he was seventeen. When he was discovered, he had a note pinned to him that said he was born in 1812. All the boy could remember was spending his life in a prison that was so small he could touch the sides. He was fed by a human who also changed his clothes and cut his nails and hair. He sat all of the time, never saw the outdoors or any other human being, and had no idea these things even existed. His keeper apparently also schooled him in numbers and letters.

When Kaspar was found, it was estimated that he had the mind of a three-year-old. He eventually learned to speak and, as his mind matured, began to realize what had

4. Ibid.

been done to him. He had missed knowing parents, family, and friendships. Probably fearing that Kaspar might remember too much, someone had him assassinated in 1833, when he was twenty-one.

Feral children remind us of the importance of the quality of human contact in children's lives. We are living in a culture of broken homes, abusive parents, latchkey kids, fathers and/or mothers absent through high-powered careers, and parents trapped by self-centeredness and unwanted children. The fact that children grow up around people certainly guarantees that they will develop into human persons. But what kind of persons? The body human—with its weaknesses, its long maturation span, and its strengths related to personhood—gives each child the opportunity for becoming a whole person. For too many children the time and potential are wasted by a wretched family environment in which morality, attitudes, beliefs, and ways of living are never transferred. Then television and peer groups play the role of heritage giver, and we raise a race of civilized feral children.

5 Rising to the Occasion

Man is the only creature with both hands and feet.

One of the most remarkable characteristics of the body human is its erect posture. Our ability to walk on two limbs, which we so easily take for granted, is not the result of a four-legged animal's acquiring small anatomical modifications and suddenly deciding to walk erect. The human upright stance is not a matter of decision but of design. Our ability to stand up and walk upright is dependent upon the arrangement of numerous anatomical and physiological features in our bodies, most of them not found in any animal. These features include the unique human foot, knees that lock, a specialized pelvis, powerful hip muscles, a sharply curved spine, and a circulatory system designed to function against gravity.

An upright posture affords us the opportunity to place our extraordinary hands at the service of our fertile minds. The wealth of human culture and the monumental successes and sins of human history have been the additive result of mind plus hand. Without our erect stance, there could not have been a human history but only unfulfilled thoughts and ideals. The mind's ability to form intricate thought patterns and to unify experiential knowledge also

119

demands rising up and engaging the world in a massive sensory encounter, not just with wet nose and dusty paws, but with uplifted eyes and searching, grasping, sensitive fingers. Condemn a Hitler or an Einstein to walk on all fours and neither foul nor great deeds would emerge. Certainly the mind's need for hands free to explore explains the baby crawler's resolute campaign to walk, though the precarious first steps result in falls, pain, and fear. Each step is really a fall forward, with no guarantee of a safe landing. This initial toddler enterprise seems so much more time- and energy-consuming than the highly polished crawl of the infant. But the exploding child's mind demands to stare at life above the horizon and not just on the carpet—to use fingers, not for merely pushing past dirt, but for manipulating all of the household goods while on the run. When our crawling children rise up and become toddlers, they are much more of a threat to the vulnerable plants and pictures decorating our tables and bookcases. As long as they crawl, our homes are baby-proof. Once crawlers stand up and walk, even the pets move aside for human dominance, which is in the form of searching, grasping, and pulling little hands.

The apes, which many consider to have nearly achieved erect posture and bipedalism, are fast and efficient "knuckle walkers," because their bodies are designed for horizontal, not upright, movement. The child, on the other hand, is poorly designed to crawl with any speed or to locomote on feet and hands. Observations of the Reverend Singh's wolf girls, who moved on hands and feet, made it clear that human beings were not designed to run on all fours. With palms down and backs high in the air, they raced along behind their wolf family, but the unnaturalness of their walking on all fours was more than obvious in arms too short, legs too long, and arm and upper-body strength woefully inadequate to support their bodies. Similarly, we have all seen tiny dogs or great tigers that walk on their hind limbs as part of a circus act. We applaud, realizing that this posture is unsteady and uncomfortable for four-legged animals. The funny, makeshift gait is evidence enough of the animal's anatomy not being a willing partner in this performance.

The speed and power of the animal world's quadrupedal posture makes me wonder what, according to evolutionary thinking, was the physical advantage of an upright posture for any of nature's animals. How could the unforeseen cultural advantage of hands being freed up to explore and work offset the immediate loss of the speed and efficiency of the four-legged world? Very few of nature's animals have to depend on two feet for survival. When they do, there is always more than adequate compensation. Birds walk erect, of course, because there is no other choice for two-legged creatures, but flying, not walking, is their gift. Penguins, whose wings and feet become paddles and rudders, are also as efficient in swimming as any fish in the sea. On land the penguin waddles humorously and very inefficiently. The kangaroo is an interesting animal, with an erect posture of sorts. Its stance is maintained only because its huge tail acts as a counterbalance to keep the kangaroo upright. Efficient motion is gained through large, violent hops. But we must struggle to see any immediate physical advantage in the human being's loss of quadrupedal mobility. Man in history is a hunter, yet without the skills or speed of a carnivore. Nature did not "experiment" with upright posture in man and stumble upon its great success. There are no signs of gradual approximations of uprightness in either primates or fossil man. Nature would not and did not take that path to the two-legged primate. And yet we walk upright.

Stand Up Like a Man

The ability for prolonged bipedal standing and walking is clearly unique to the human being. Without certain ana-tomical adjustments, the upright stance is unwieldy and clumsy in four-legged animals. This unwieldiness is even more pronounced in walking. In order to stand, the tall, thin human body must be balanced. In order to walk, the body must continuously shift its center of gravity from side to side in maintaining that delicate balance. Even with a body designed to perform this balancing act, a baby still has difficulty learning to walk upright. Animals whose bodies are designed for quadrupedal movement can manage uprightness for only short, difficult periods of time. The act of walking is so effortless and smooth for us that we fail to consider the anatomical uniqueness that makes it possible.

By way of comparison, the gorilla's anatomy reveals its design for a quadrupedal knuckle-walking posture, which, indeed, is the major form of locomotion for the gorilla. The gorilla's pelvic region is very long and tilted forward to pro-duce its bent-over stance, whereas our pelvis is short and upright. The gorilla's shoulder girdle is more massive than our own, making it top-heavy and unwieldy on two legs. The gorilla's arms are much larger than its legs (the opposite ratio to the human being's), making possible the knuckle-walking position. The gorilla's foot not only has no arch support, but it is anatomically more similar to its own hand than to the superbly designed human foot. Because of the large size of the gorilla's head and the rear entry point of the spine into the skull base, its head hangs for-ward, supported by massive neck muscles. This is to be contrasted with our own head, balanced on the top of the spine and requiring only a thin, highly flexible neck as support. In general, the human being is less top-heavy, with a lower, more stabilizing center of gravity than the gorilla. It is clear that a multitude of unique engineering changes in the human anatomy prepare the body for upright posture and bipedal walking.

Although the apes are able to stand up and balance on their hind limbs, they do so only for brief periods of time. If they attempt to walk and maintain this balance, they appear very clumsy indeed. With the exception of the gibbon, apes normally walk in a quadrupedal position, with their weight supported on the sides of their feet and the knuckles of their fingers. The protracted arms and truncated legs of the apes give them a diagonal, semi-erect stance. This posture is called semi-erect to emphasize that the stance of the large apes contrasts rather sharply with the erect bipedalism of man. Semi-erect quadrupedalism is not even a comfortable possibility for us humans. Our short arms and long legs would only do for a humorous four-legged race after the sack race at the church picnic. Actually, the quadrupedalism of an ape differs very little from that of other animals. The major difference is that the ape's upper body is poised higher.

Of all the apes, the slightly built gibbon has the most human-looking walk. In the zoo the gibbon is the small ape that will walk upright across the ground or, more usually, on a horizontal branch of a tree, with its long arms held high and wide as balancers. Out of the trees the gibbon's arms would drag on the ground if it did not hold them aloft. On the ground the gibbon races on the flat of its feet, more like a man. But in the trees its weight rests on the front part of the foot, which grasps the tree limb like a hand. Similar as this may seem to the human stance, we must realize that this is an artificial mode of locomotion for the gibbon. The gibbon normally does not descend from the trees, and the tree branches rarely provide horizontal platforms for this type of walking.

Apes do have a different form of gait from the monkeys because of some important anatomical differences. Apes have short, wide, shallow trunks that cannot bend. They have long, free-swinging arms that can reach out in all directions, enabling the apes to play Tarzan and swing from branch to branch in the trees, instead of running on all fours on the tops of branches like the monkeys.

These anatomical differences do not, however, make the apes bipedal animals like man. Apes are still four-legged animals. Their anatomical features offer them the advantage of a wide variety of movement patterns on the ground other than the four-legged run of the monkey. The extremely long-armed gorilla and chimpanzee are knuckle-walkers. The orangutan is unhandy at best on the ground and spends all its time in the trees. The gibbon is fun to watch on the ground, gingerly running bent-kneed along a narrow line, with hands held high. The apes differ from monkeys from the waist up, but—to achieve fully erect bipedalism like man—apes would need changes from the waist down characteristic of man. Our erect posture depends primarily upon the structure of the human pelvis, knees, and feet.

There is little basis for comparison between humans and monkeys in terms of the anatomy of movement. Monkeys are quadrupeds and very similar to other four-legged mammals in basic anatomy. The trunk of the monkey's body is long and narrow and deep, much like that of the dog. Simulating the action of a dog's limbs, the monkey keeps its limbs parallel, movement being limited largely to a backward and forward plane. Because of this arrangement, a monkey, like a dog, will stretch by reaching forward. Monkeys in the trees will run along the tops of branches in a way similar to four-legged animals on the ground.

Monkeys have extremely flexible trunks, suitable for their rapid acrobatic running on the branches. The apes, on the other hand, are solidly built as tree climbers, even though they spend much of their time on the ground. They have tremendous upper-body strength and long, powerful arms. Built for activity overhead in the trees, the gorilla's shoulder blades extend upward. Monkeys' shoulder blades are almost parallel to each other on the sides of the rib cage. Our own shoulder blades are on our upper back. Lumbar vertebrae (those with no ribs attached) usually number six or seven in monkeys, three in most apes, and normally five in humans. There is therefore considerable flexibility in the monkey and human trunks and almost none at all in most apes. The monkey has a tilted pelvis for the attachment of leg muscles, whereas the gorilla's pelvis provides a base for muscles to support its heavily stooped trunk. Our pelvis, though, uniquely supports the upper body and is an excellent base for the powerful muscles used in walking.

The origins of these bipedal features in man are a mystery. No family line can be safely drawn anatomically from monkeys or apes to men. Even fossil man shows every indication of having had a similar walking anatomy to modern man and a fully erect bipedal posture. Jacob Bronowski observed, "Two million years ago, the first certain ancestor of man walked with a foot which is almost indistinguishable from the foot of modern man."[1] There are doubts about when fossil man walked the earth, but there is no doubt about the type of foot he walked on. Mary Leakey and her co-workers provided support for the same

---

1. Jacob Bronowski, *The Ascent of Man* (Boston: Little Brown and Co., 1973) p. 28.

view with a discovery of four-million-year-old human footprints found at Laetolil, Northern Tanzania.[2] We can conclude that fossil man cannot be considered a "bridge" between quadrupedalism in animals and bipedalism in modern man.

Let us now look more in detail at some of the unique features behind the human's erect posture.

The Foot

At the end of a long day of teaching, my feet hurt. Perhaps my shoes are the problem. They feel comfortable, but standing is hard work. A few weeks ago, while at the zoo, my family and I spent several minutes staring at a chimpanzee who had decided to sit close to the fence that separated us. As "human" as the chimp might have appeared at first glance, something about him seemed out of place. At the bottom of his legs, which were lying in front of him, were his feet, but they did not look like feet at all. He had a short "big" toe, clearly separated from his other toes, which bent under and inward. His other toes were exceptionally long and also sharply curved downward in the direction of the big toe. What I was staring at was not a foot like mine, but something much more akin to the chimpanzee's hand. It is no wonder he was sitting down. I could not imagine teaching all day on my hands. They were not designed for that. The chimpanzee got up and clearly grasped a branch with his "foot." It functioned better as a hand than a foot. More than any other part of the body, more than even the skull, it is the foot that so readily identifies man as man to a fossil hunter. Human feet, as the twin bases of support for our upright posture, are com-

2. M. D. Leakey and R. L. Hay, "Pliocene Footprints in the Laetolil beds at Laetolil, Northern Tanzania," *Nature*, 1979, *278*, 317–323.

pletely unique in the animal world. In fact, man is the only creature who has both hands and feet.

All animals with four limbs have either four hands or four feet. Man, on the contrary, has two functional supporting feet and two completely different and highly proficient hands. Primates do not have the benefit of real feet to walk on. Their "feet" are suited for life in the trees, whereas man's feet are needed for erect, bipedal movement. It is an oversimplification to talk about slight modifications made in the primate "foot" in order to develop the human foot. Massive, not slight, differences distinguish primate and human feet. When I was viewing pictures in an anatomy book that compared human and primate feet, my two-year-old son climbed excitedly into

There is a remarkable similarity between the chimp's hands and feet.

my lap to see the book. Before I could tell him what he was looking at, he pointed to a picture of a gorilla foot and said, "Hand." Admittedly, this is not an empirical way to determine whether or not primates have feet, but it does show how our ordinary experience of what is a foot or a hand has been too easily dismissed—not by scientific data, but by the need to relate apes to men. My son's casual observation about gorilla feet is more than amply supported by a more rigorous comparison of human and primate feet.[3]

The architecture of the human foot, particularly of the arch and the big toe, is unique. The human foot seems primarily designed as a bony support for the completely upright standing-and-walking human body. Better than metal, bone is the perfect material for overall support and flexibility of the body, particularly in the foot, which has to provide strong, light, and flexible support. This support function is further aided by the fact that the muscles of the human foot have little to do with moving it. The foot is moved primarily by muscles in the leg. The foot has almost as many muscles as the hand, but these are not called on to make the fine, delicate movements of a hand. The monkey or ape foot, though, can make many small, precise movements of grasping with its musculature. The human foot is equipped for standing and walking, and the work of its muscles is confined largely to supporting the bones that form the all-important arch and, to a lesser extent, to wiggling and stretching the toes.

The human foot is unique in that it has a lightweight arch for strong support. The arch absorbs the shock of walking as the weight is constantly being shifted from foot

3. J. Lessertisseur and F. K. Jouffroy, "Comparative Osteometry of the Foot of Man and Facultatively Bipedal Primates," in Russell H. Tuttle (ed.), *Primate Functional Morphology and Evolution* (Paris: Mouton Publishers, 1975) pp. 327–340.

to foot. People without significant foot arches ("flat feet") have painful walking after a while, since the unabsorbed jars of motion are eventually transmitted up the spinal column to the skull. Apes do not have arches, and upright walking is consequently difficult for them. The ankles also give stability to the stance and, when a person is walking, carry the weight of the body from the ankles and heel through the balls and toes of the foot. When we take a step, our cushioned heel lands first, followed by the ball of the foot and the toes. The big toe then moves to provide the forward thrust of the next step. The rigid arches keep the points of contact at a minimum. Since the apes have no "big" toe as such (theirs is shorter than the other toes), they walk with their feet bent. Their ankles and the sides of their feet touch the ground, rather than the heels and balls of the feet, and this produces a shuffling stride. Humans, therefore, have longer strides than apes, are capable of more speed bipedally, and stand and walk with a lot less energy expenditure.

In comparison with the apes, our foot is short with respect to our legs, with a long heel bone, very short external toes, and a very long big toe. The big toe is not unusually large except as it compared to the other toes, which have a greatly reduced size. Only in the human foot are the small toes parallel to and attached to the big toe by a ligament, so that the front of the foot seems to be almost one piece. In the course of walking, the big toe supports all by itself nearly one-half of the forces transmitted to the length of the foot.

Of the apes, gibbons and orangutans have the best grasp with their feet, but chimpanzees and gorillas have a very good grasp as well. Gorillas, though, which are the most terrestrial of the apes, have their big toes closer and more in line with their other toes than do the other apes. The mountain gorilla, the most terrestrial of the gorillas, has this adaptation the most. But its foot can still grasp well and is no further along toward a real foot in any other feature, except possibly in the strength of its big toe. The gorilla's big toe is stronger than the other apes'. The orangutan, by comparison, has a tiny "big" toe and its terminal joint and toenail are often missing. The flexor muscles of the orangutan's big toe are comparatively weak, and it climbs by using mostly the second to the fifth digits to grip branches.

The Knee

To get an idea of the major benefit of the knee for the human posture, we need merely visit an army post and observe soldiers standing in formation. Soldiers may stand in rigid formation for long periods of time before they tire because of the knee's ability to fix the leg in a straight rather than bent position. In this locked position, the energy expenditure is almost nothing when compared to the bent-knee position of the ape. Muscles of the thigh and hip do not have to work to support the weight of the human body in this position.

The human knee joint, in conjunction with muscles in the lower limb, is able to lock the leg in a permanently straight, restful position. The important knee joint is protected by a separate bone called the patella or "knee bone," a small, flat bone that is not connected to any other bone. It is held in place rather loosely by a muscle attachment above and below and thus seems to float over the top of the knee joint.

The Pelvis

Of all the mammals, only in the human being do the hipbones form such a rounded and bowl-like structure. The abdominal organs of four-legged animals hang from the backbone and are supported ventrally by the muscular wall of the abdomen. But, in erect human beings, the abdominal wall is vertical and cannot provide support for the internal organs. Therefore, the human pelvis (Latin for "basin") is rounded to give some support for these organs. Since the pelvis is tipped forward, the support is only partial.

An analysis of the pelvic girdle of a skeleton will tell us whether it was male or female, since the female pelvis must leave room for a developing fetus. Her pelvic bones are thinner and lighter and approximately two inches wider than the male's. Her pelvis is also rounder and more spacious. Because of its wider shape, the angle made by the meeting of the two pubic bones is wider in the female, where it is about ninety degrees. In the male, the angle is only seventy degrees. Women, therefore, have comparatively larger hips and sway when they walk. They also have more difficulty in running, since their wider hips are further from the center of gravity and cause their knees to point inward slightly. We can expect the fastest women sprinters to be those with relatively narrow hips.

In the pelvis of the body human, major morphological distinctions are found in direct relation to bipedal motion. The ilium bone extends farther back in humans, which puts the hip muscles into a different alignment with the hip joint. This new alignment adapts the hip muscles' functions to bipedal walking. These hip muscles, the gluteus maximus and gluteus medius, form what we politely call "buns." Whether we like it or not, we have much larger buns than the apes because of the requirements of our upright posture. Apes and monkeys are animals with tremendous upper-body strength but are small-bottomed. Monkeys who spend a lot of time sitting in trees have large ischial callosites, or sitting pads, to sit on in the absence of the cushion we humans enjoy. In the human pelvis the iliac crest is also much larger than in primates, giving a more extensive attachment for the muscles used in supporting the trunk in the erect posture. Our buttock muscles also serve to pull the body forward and over the leg with each stride. The gorilla, with underdeveloped buttock muscles, can manage at best only a shuffle.

The Upper Body

Apes are designed for brachiating through the trees, which requires enormous upper-body strength and exceptionally long arms. A chimpanzee of a hundred pounds would be several times stronger in that respect than the average man. When we watch a chimpanzee swing in a zoo cage, we should recall our own attempts to do chin-ups on a bar. Tarzan would never have been able to follow apes and monkeys through the trees. Unlike his ape friends, Tarzan's collar bones, like ours, were positioned horizontally and correlated with a more efficient use of his arms below the shoulder level and not above the shoulders in the trees. In fact, no animal can swim the free-style stroke because animal limbs cannot rotate completely around like ours.

Our arms and trunk are short as compared to our legs, which is just the reverse of primates. The advantages of this form for upright walking are stronger legs and a less top-heavy frame for better balance during the upright posture. Our long legs are unique. The thigh bone is the longest bone in the body, making up two-sevenths of the height of the body. The tibia (shinbone) is the second largest bone of the body. A comparison of the body proportions of various primates shows the singularity of the human design. The arm-leg ratio ($\times$ 100) for the macaque monkey is approximately 112, gibbon 165, orangutan 172, chimpanzee 136, gorilla 138, man 80.[4] These proportions would make us a comical sight if we tried to walk on all fours, whereas it is a natural position for the apes. Gorillas and chimpanzees rest their weight on the knuckles of the second to the fifth digits of each hand, and the skin in these areas is thickened and calloused. The orangutans rarely walk on the ground, but when they do, they place their palms flat or make a fist on the ground. Electromyography studies (implant electrodes in various muscles and record) show that when the gorilla is in a knuckle-walking position, there is very little electrical activity in the muscles that flex the fingers and the muscles that counteract the bent hand.[5] This suggests that it is the close packing of the wrist bones and the arrangement of ligaments in the hand that keep the gorilla hand in the knuckle-walking position. Thus, knuckle-walking seems to be a "natural" position for a gorilla. The chimpanzee's hand also seems built for knuckle-walking, since its wrist will bend only thirty degrees backwards, whereas an orangutan, not a knuckle-walker, can bend its wrist eighty-five degrees backwards.[6]

Humans are also considerably less top-heavy than the apes. For example, our skulls are small and light. By contrast, the head of the gorilla, as well as its supporting musculature, is so massive that the skull is not uniformly a solid structure. The skull and facial region contain an extensive system of sinuses, particularly in older large males, and these serve to reduce the skull's weight. With a less massive chest, humans have a lower center of gravity,

4. A. F. Dixson, *The Natural History of the Gorilla* (London: Weidenfeld and Nicolson, 1981) p. 36.

5. Ibid., p. 40.

6. Ibid.

closer to the fulcrum of the hip joint, and more of our
weight is transmitted to our heels. Therefore, we are less
in danger of falling flat on our faces because of top-
heaviness. The ape's center of gravity is high and forward.
With relatively weak legs, the apes must elevate and maintain erect posture at a greater mechanical disadvantage as
compared to human beings.

The human spinal column is also essential for an upright posture. The spine or backbone can bend in all directions because it is a column of separate bones (vertebrae)
joined together by thick bonds of tissue. The top seven vertebrae are the neck bones; the ribs are attached to the next
twelve; and then there are two bones made of several
vertebrae grown together. Disks and cartilage act as
cushions between the vertebrae, keeping them from rub-
bing against each other and protecting the brain from the
jolts of running and walking.

The human spine has four sharp curves in the form of a
double-S shape, in contrast to the straight spine or gentle
backward curve of all animals. This shape of spine allows
us to be comfortable in a wide variety of body positions, a
fact of importance to a creature of many and varied activities. The double-S column, which bends backwards in the
region of the hip, makes the erect posture an easier one to
maintain and gives us a springy balance. The lumbar vertebrae (near the bottom of the column) are the largest and
heaviest of the spinal column and are well equipped to
support our upright posture. The gorilla spine, like that of
other quadrupeds, is fairly straight as compared to ours
and does not assist the gorilla in an upright posture. The
lumbar region of the gorilla spine is shorter than in
human beings, with very little curvature and no thickened vertebrae.

The Neck

The body human's spine enters the skull through the foramen magnum, a hole located in the center of the skull's base—unlike all other primate entry points, which are located to the rear of the skull's base. This portion of the human spine leaves the human head balanced neatly on the neck. With balance assured, our neck muscles are small, giving us a graceful, flexible neck. Unlike the apes, we can turn our heads easily without turning our upper torsos, whereas the neck of the gorilla is virtually non-existent. Head movement is very important to the active human being, who has so much to see and do. The human spine enters the foramen magnum at a slight angle from the front, an arrangement that further increases the flexibility of the human neck. The ape head, though, hangs rigidly and heavily from the spine, rather than sitting on it. The skull of an infant of the large apes actually looks more human than the adult ape's skull, since its foramen magnum opens more directly downwards. As a result, the foramen magnum lies underneath the infant ape's skull rather than at the posterior end. As the infant skull grows, though, the opening shifts progressively backwards. We are unique in that our foramen magnum remains under the cranium throughout life.

Since the adult gorilla's head is so massive, it must be held in position by larger neck muscles than ours. The neck vertebrae of gorillas show special adaptation for these large neck muscles by having enlarged dorsal spines for muscle attachment. Because of the neck spines and the extra-large neck muscles, a gorilla cannot look over its shoulder but needs to turn the whole front of its body around. Of course, the gorilla probably does not have to worry about anyone sneaking up from behind.

Circulatory System

The upright stance of the human being requires a major modification of the circulatory system. We will faint if the heart is not well supplied with blood and the brain is cut off from its sufficient supply. Since a large amount of the blood flow to the heart comes from the feet, legs, and abdomen, a standing person's blood must be pumped against gravity to reach the heart. Sometimes the blood has to be lifted as much as four or five feet. Many animals lack the ability to overcome the negative effects of gravity on their blood flow. The rabbit, for example, if held upright for too long, will die because its blood collects of its own weight in the great veins of the abdomen, until insufficient blood is entering the heart. Sheep held upright during too long a shearing will often die for a similar reason. The blood nearly drains out of the heart of a snake that is suspended vertically. The great apes and dogs, however, do have some measure of circulatory compensation for a vertical stance. Only the body human, though, has a superbly designed circulatory system that perfectly adjusts to the vertical stance.

The human circulatory system adjusts to the vertical posture in a variety of ways. When we stand up, a reflex occurs in which vasoconstrictor nerves reduce substantially the capacity of peripheral blood vessels. Blood thus flows more easily to the heart instead of collecting in the abdominal region. Also, when we are standing, the muscles of our abdominal wall automatically contract and firmly support the great veins of the abdominal cavity to prevent them from collecting blood. A third helpful feature of the human circulatory system is that it contains valves that open upward but not downward, which provides additional support to blood flowing against gravity. When we stand, a fourth circulatory adjustment is made as our leg muscles contract and exert a squeezing force on the veins lying between them. Blood is thereby driven up-hill toward the heart but cannot return because of the one-way valves. Finally, our normal breathing movements propel blood upward toward the heart in two ways. First, every intake of breath lowers the pressure within the tho-rax, which is already lower than that of the atmosphere to which the rest of the body is exposed. This pressure change pushes the blood toward the heart with each breath. Second, the descent of the diaphragm during each breath increases the intra-abdominal pressure, which also forces blood upward but not downward, again because of the one-way valves.

Since apes do not possess the same degree of compensa-tion by the circulatory system for an upright posture, their experience during a lengthy bipedal stance must be very uncomfortable. When we rise up out of bed suddenly, we may experience light-headedness because blood has col-lected in our abdomen and lower limbs. Blood pressure drops as soon as we stand, since gravity begins to counter blood flow to the heart, although our normal standing re-flexes quickly clear our consciousness. Since the apes must experience this problem frequently, they consequently do not spend more than a few seconds bipedally before bend-ing back down to the ground, if only for a few seconds. Para-lyzed humans, especially those with high spinal lesions, may frequently have drops in blood pressure when they are moved to an upright posture. Here the problem is the absence of muscle tension, and their bodies cannot adjust adequately to having to move blood against gravity.

The Human Hand

The major benefit of our upright mobility is that the hands are freed to do the work of the mind and to help us pursue a more active manipulation and exploration of the world. Our ability to develop personally depends on our ability to give the sense of touch to thought. Human life is more than hands catching rabbits or gathering fruit to eat. If that were all that mattered, then a carnivore's mouth or an elephant's trunk would have been sufficient, even superior. We would not expect nature to give up four walking limbs and their speed and power, just for rabbit stew. The body human has been designed, however, to facilitate the development of personal contact, culture, applied reason, and aesthetic construction. The spectra of culture, art, libraries, architecture, war, space travel, medicine, games, theater, and romance are all supported by a body that stands up and reaches out.

With its upright stance a human being has the capability of combining a long attention span, wide-angle stereoscopic vision, and an exquisite hand with truly opposable thumbs. While many monkeys have stereoscopic vision, it is only in man that there exists the powerful combination of visual skills, attentive abilities, and a talented hand—all necessary for close-in, prolonged eye-hand coordination. It takes a lot of cortical control to attend with eye control to a small object like a needle, to precisely move thread toward the needle, and to do this for a lengthy period of time. This does not mean that it is easy for me to thread a needle, but it is impossible for chimpanzees or gorillas, even if they had the desire to do so. With this ability we can pick up tiny pins, hold heavy saws, turn doorknobs, finger computer or piano keys, tickle, untie, pluck, paint, catch, signal, and more.

When we twist our hands or wiggle our fingers, there are

twenty-seven small bones in each hand and wrist that slip and move together as a loose unit. The fifty-four bones of our two hands comprise over one-fourth of the two hundred and six bones in the whole body. Each wrist has eight bones that can slide a bit over each other, creating the wrist's flexibility for a wide variety of movements. The palm of our hands may look like one bone, but it is actually five fingerlike bones. The thumb base is set at an angle to the other four bones of the palm, so that the thumb can move toward the other fingers. The bones of the palm are loosely connected to increase the flexibility of our grip. The reason why a skeleton's fingers look so long is that each "finger" of the skeleton is actually a finger bone plus a palm bone, which together look frighteningly long. Thirty muscles move the bones of each hand. The brain's cortical areas devoted to controlling these muscles are larger than the combined areas that control the chest and abdomen. Arm muscles also contribute to hand movement. The muscles on the palm side of the forearm bend the fingers and wrist and turn the hand palm down. The muscles on the other side of the forearm straighten the fingers, pull the hand back at the wrist, and turn the hand palm up.

The dermis of the palm is ridged (as are the soles of the feet) with small parallel lines that extend with artistic, gentle curves. On the tips of the fingers these ridges form whirls and loops. Like tire treads, these ridges, which run counter to the direction of gripping motion, strengthen the grip by increasing the surface area and consequently the friction between hand and object. Tiny drops of sweat and oil produced in the palms further enhance the gripping capability of the hands. The digits of apes and even the tails of some monkeys also have "fingerprints." Our fingerprints are so individualized that no two human beings, not even identical twins, will have the same markings, which develop into permanent patterns during the third or fourth month of fetal development.

Hand skin is exquisitely sensitive, in spite of the fact that the top layer (the epidermis) is dead and insensitive. This layer of dead cells is thin enough that the nerve endings in the dermis are able to interact with the world and supply rich sensitivity for the stimulus-hungry brain.

Fingernails and toenails are horny outgrowths of skin, yet hardly qualify as weapons like the fearsome claws of carnivores. Fingernails offer thin, hard surfaces for delicate tasks such as picking up small objects.

Primate adaptations for gripping things are variable. Of the sixty-five species of the New World monkeys, many have a fifth hand, the tail, which is not present in Old World counterparts. The most arboreal of the apes, the brachiating gibbons and orangutans, have long, strong fingers that flex into hooks for swinging in the trees. The short thumbs of these primates are actually kept out of the way when the owners are swinging, and they serve only minor purpose in the hands' function. The marmoset has the most primitive grip of all the monkeys, since all of its fingers move in the same plane. The only opposability it can obtain from its hands is to press an object against the heel of its hand. The macaque monkey and the chimpanzee have the most dexterous hands of the primates. Both can pick up small objects between thumb and finger. The chimpanzee's thumb is shorter and thus less efficient than the macaque's, but its brain is considerably better, enabling the chimpanzee to be far more skillful with its hand. It is the prosimian potto that has the best opposition of thumb to finger of any primate. Instead of a full index finger, the potto has only a vestigial stump, which strengthens the potto's grip. The gorilla and the chimpanzee have a longer thumb than the other apes, but its tip does not extend to the proximal crease of the index finger. In apes the thumb is also less capable of opposing with strength, because the tendon of the flexor pollicis muscle is reduced or absent. Actually, one of the best opposable thumbs in the animal world may be that of the giant panda who has six digits per paw. The panda's thumb is not anatomically a finger at all, but an extension of one of its wrist bones.

For humans the case is different. Our thumbs are the strongest finger we have, which is why those handy tacks are called "thumb" tacks. Our thumb is also completely opposable, thanks to its length, shorter fingers, and the thumb's independent plane of movement. We have no difficulty touching each finger with our long thumb. The ease with which this is possible makes our hands the finest grasping mechanism of any primate.

The combination of upright posture, grasping hand, and imaginative mind have made possible the elaborate use of hand tools for our culture building. A few other animals have acquired the use of tools, but the skill is very elementary. Chimpanzees, for example, throw rocks or threaten and strike with hand-held clubs. Chimpanzees also make extensive use of twigs to pull termites out of their mounds and also use leaves to chew with food or to wipe themselves if a bowel movement occasionally soils them.

Tool use in primates, though impressive, falls short of even the most rudimentary tool use by man. Human tool manufacture usually involves much foresight, and materials are collected over a wide area distant from the place of eventual use. This was true even of so-called fossil man. Humans rely constantly and extensively on tools. In the life of a chimpanzee, tools are a rarity, and the chimpanzee does not need them for continued survival. Humans also use tools to make other tools. Chimpanzees do not, apparently because using tools to make tools requires advanced mental abilities.

The Human Combination

Standing up has never been a popular pasttime. Lying down, sitting, and resting have gotten all the publicity. But standing up and reaching out should remind us of our humanness. When we stand to honor a person entering the room, that is humanness. When we "rise to the occasion" during trying times, that is humanness. When we "lend someone a hand," or talk of "handling" our problems, that is humanness. Only man, because of his unique bodily posture, is freed to be fully "human." The body human is so much of my foundation that it becomes indistinguishable from who I am. I am my hands and my feet. I am the arches of thumb to finger and heel to toe.

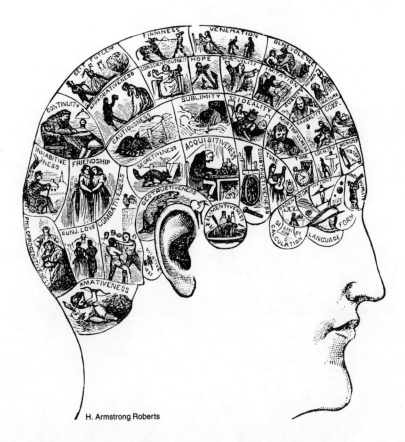

H. Armstrong Roberts

The Matter of Mind

Man is the only creature with a preference for the right hand.

The human brain is a mysterious loom, weaving the strands of billions of neuronal dendrites into the fabric of thought itself. Perhaps the neurochemical threads blend with invisible threads of spirit to form the essence of personhood. Or perhaps something more profound and unknowable occurs. There is probably nothing to be found in the universe that is more complicated than the human brain. In fact, all of our hopes of understanding it or ourselves may rest on this question: "Can my brain possibly understand my brain?"

In looking for those areas where humans differ from animals, I find that the brain is certainly rich with discovery. Both dualists and materialists agree that we are somehow up there behind our eyes, inside our head. Since we are so different from animals, it is inside the brain where the major differences must reside.

The brain is a swarm of cells in which everything is seemingly connected to everything else. The connections, though, follow a plan, an order, the large elements of which we are just beginning to see and understand. The charmed cell of the brain is the neuron, whose exact numbers are difficult to calculate, but ten billion is an often-quoted figure. The actual number may be ten times that. The brain is also made of much smaller glial cells, whose functions are unclear. Numbering ten times the neurons, they comprise half the volume of the brain. Human neurons are small cells of .5–20 microns in diameter (micron = $^1\!/_{1000}$ of a millimeter). Brain neurons, for the most part, are only slightly longer than wide, but neurons throughout the body may reach several feet in length. Neurons, bundled up to make nerves, run from the foot to the base of the spine, a distance of several feet. As small as they are, brain neurons stretched end to end would reach to the moon and back several times. Each neuron is capable of sending electrical signals down its length in the form of a chemical leak of sodium and potassium. The electrical signal is passed from one neuron to the next over a small synaptic cleft via chemicals known as transmitters. Each neuron may contact thousands of others over synapses, thus making a mind-boggling possible number of interconnections in the brain. The electrical activity of the neuron, or nerve impulse, travels at a respectable 100 meters per second, or about 225 miles per hour. Such a speed is fast but not instantaneous. The tail-to-head distance in the blue whale is over a hundred feet. Therefore, a small amount of time elapses before a whale feels the harpoon hit its tail. Since thousands of interconnections may grace a single synapse, it is clear that the living brain is a buzzing electrical network.

The brain appears on the outside to be a wrinkled mass of gray, spongy-looking matter. What we are looking at is the cerebral cortex, which covers almost the entire brain. The cortex resembles a twenty-square-foot tablecloth, stuffed, squeezed, and folded around a grapefruit. The resulting wrinkles, or convolutions, in the human cortex are much more ordered than in the tablecloth, but they serve the obvious purpose of increasing the surface area of the valuable cortex. Only about one-third of the surface area of the cerebral cortex is visible, with the other two-thirds buried within the valleys (sulci) of the cortex. The great size of the cortex, which distinguishes the human from the animal brains, is related to our humanness.

The cerebral cortex is involved with sensory and motor functions. Cells that receive incoming information from all of the senses except smell are located in the posterior two-thirds of the cortex. Visual cortex, for example, is located at the very back of the brain, and its 10-percent share of cortex indicates the importance of vision to us. The control of muscle movement, speech, memory, and the not-well-understood thinking process also resides in the cortex. Under the cortex are regions of the brain that handle emotion, motivation, and smell. The lowest portion of the brain regulates vital functions such as breathing and heart rate and contains an activation center to alert the cortex to incoming information.

The importance of the brain to body function is seen in the fact that it receives 25 to 30 percent of the blood flow from the heart, and it receives it continuously. Other parts of the body receive varying amounts of blood according to their needs and other body-area needs—but not the brain. Unable to store its own fuel or extract energy without oxygen, the brain needs a constant supply of blood. A one-second interruption of blood flow uses up the dissolved oxygen in the brain. A two-minute interruption begins permanent damage to the brain.

The Uniqueness of Man's Brain

Since our brain is considerably larger than most animal brains, it would be tempting to assume that the major difference between a human and any other animal lies in the quantity of brain cells. We should not yield to that temptation, though, for it is clear that it is the presence of rich, new interconnections of nervous tissue that gives rise to the major qualitative differences between man and animals. It is not the quantity of interconnections per se, but the arrangement of neurons into new and unique brain areas, that contributes to unique human abilities. The frontal lobes, the left-hemisphere speech center, and the association cortex are examples of such areas. These areas do not by themselves constitute the person, but they are an exceedingly valuable tool in the formation and expression of humanness.

Elephants (5,000 grams) and whales (6,800 grams) have the largest brains on the planet, but they are clearly not the most intelligent animals. Women have brains that are 10-percent smaller than men's, and yet they are not 10-percent less intelligent. The existence of a wide range of normal human brain sizes (from 900 to 2,000 grams), without any relationship to intelligence, suggests that brain size per se is not the distinguishing human factor.

It might be suggested that it is not just brain size but brain size relative to body size that determines intelligence and humanness. Thus, if a whale's huge brain is utilizing all of its mass to control its huge body, then very little brain is left to compose poetry. But again we must remember that the human body can vary considerably in weight with no variance in people's intelligence. Although the human brain/body ratio is high (1/50) when compared to the elephant (1/1000), chimpanzee (1/150), or gorilla (1/500), there are higher brain/body ratios in the animal world. Small monkeys (such as the capuchin monkey) and hummingbirds are under a 1/20 brain/body ratio. The dwarf monkeys of South America, the marmosets, have one gram of brain to every gram of body. Therefore, we know that some quantity of brain and a low brain/body ratio is helpful to intelligence, but we need to dispel the idea that by increasing the size of the gorilla brain, we would have a man. The problem of biologists is not to explain how larger brains developed, but how complex structures appeared fully developed in the human brain with no gradual approximations in the animal world.

The areas of the human brain that distinguish it from the animal brain are the following. First, the human brain has a massive enlargement of the frontal lobes. Second, the human brain has a massive enlargement of areas collectively known as association cortex. Third, the human brain shows some remarkable hemispheric specialization in speech, manual dexterity, and other functions. Fourth, the human brain has a unique area devoted to the production and perception of speech.

The Frontal Lobes

Approximately one-half of the volume of our cerebral cortex consists of the frontal cortex. This brain area includes the premotor and motor cortex as well as the mysterious prefrontal areas immediately behind the forehead and eyes. It is this latter area that most people have in mind when they speak of the frontal lobes. Since the prefrontal cortex barely exists in laboratory rats and mice, it has been difficult to study. In cats and dogs the prefrontal cortex makes up 3.5 and 7 percent of the cerebral cortex respectively. In chimpanzees prefrontal cortex makes up 17 percent of the cerebral cortex. Our own prefrontal cortex is most impressive—at 29 percent—almost a third of the entire cerebral cortex.[1]

1. Maya Pines, "The Human Difference," *Psychology Today*, September 1983, pp. 62–68.

Hints about the function of the frontal lobes were provided by the famous case of Phineas Gage, a competent laborer on the construction of the Rutland and Burlington Railroad in 1848. He was reported to have had a good intellect and personality. One day Phineas was tapping a drill hole full of explosives and a fuse, when they prematurely exploded. The tamping iron, which was over three feet long and one-fourth inch in diameter and weighed over thirteen pounds, was blown through Phineas's left cheek, into the skull and frontal lobes, and through the top of his head. Phineas was stunned but was able to walk normally and talk to the doctor to whom he was taken. The rod amputated the forward part of the frontal lobes on both sides, giving Phineas what was later to be called prefrontal lobotomy. After this chance lobotomy, Phineas was no longer himself. He became vulgar, obstinate, capricious, flitted from one job to another, and had trouble thinking ahead. He could not always control his passions as an adult normally does. Phineas died in 1861, stricken with convulsions.

The importance of the prefrontal lobotomy was publicized by Egas Moniz, who developed surgeries to cut the neural tracts from the frontal lobes to the thalamus. In other words, he sectioned off the frontal lobes from the rest of the brain. By the late 1940s, tens of thousands of such lobotomies had been performed in which holes were drilled on the top or the sides of the skull and varying amounts of neural tracts were disconnected. Quick transorbital lobotomies were also performed in the psychiatrist's office. Electrical shock administered to the brain was the anesthesia. Then an instrument that looked like an ice pick was driven by a mallet through the bone of the upper corner of the orbit of the eye. The pointed instrument was pushed in a measurable distance and moved from side to side to slice through frontal-lobe material. In 1949 Egas Moniz won the Nobel Prize for his efforts. Today the operation is a relic of the past because of its negative effects on the patient. At best, the operation may have produced thousands of Phineas Gages.

The emotional character of the prefrontal-lobotomy patient reveals persistent, strange periods of apathy and occasional times of euphoria. Social awareness seems absent as the patients impulsively make decisions. There is little concern for past or future. In general, the emotions are shallow, with only occasional flare-ups of exhilaration or silliness. The cognitive changes in the patient are minor but troubling. The patient has not lost IQ points but seems forgetful in situations where good attention is demanded. The patient has trouble initiating such simple activities as opening and closing the fist, but once begun, the activity is hard to stop. Movements of the patient seem "blah" and not spontaneous. The facial expression is usually blank. In daily life the patient seems disorganized. The symptoms of the lobotomized patient are confusing, but they do suggest that the frontal lobes are involved in memory functions, planning controls, and feedback and inhibitory controls on behavior.

Our frontal lobes seem to be involved with helping us to think of future actions and their consequences. Humans are normally able to fix an action or consequence at a location in the future and move toward it for a long, even uncertain, period of time. An Olympic medal-winning gymnast may have charted her single-minded course for a dozen years. A normal person who misses a bus is able to restructure present plans with a knowledge of the past and manage to get to work anyway. The frontal lobes seem to aid us in maintaining the initiative in moving along the path to a near or far goal. Large and complicated behaviors are especially disrupted without the frontal lobes. Self-awareness seems fragmentary, and decision making is hesitant. The frontal lobes also contain high levels of dopamine, a transmitter implicated in schizophrenia, a mental illness with some symptoms similar to those of prefrontal patients.

The body human's huge frontal lobes, absent in most animals and present as paltry bulges in others, add an expansive dimension to human life. Our responses to the environment are affected by our anticipations of the future. We are able to focus on both past and future as twin supports to lift our self-awareness out of present time. We are thus able to move back and forth from past memories through present ideals to future goals. We can imagine that which does not yet exist or that which will never exist. Our huge memory capacity is utilized by frontal-lobe mechanisms as a type of nongenetic inheritance to shape our future decisions. The frontal lobes are able to hold on to the past by memory traces as it moves us into the future. Man is the only creature on earth who lives as if his physical brain has allowed him to transcend the physical. And that is what it is to be human.

Association Cortex

Another area of distinction in the body human's brain is its large amount of cortical area outside of primary sensory cortex, that is, outside of areas devoted to seeing, hearing, and the sense of touch. These association areas, as they are called, are located within each hemisphere of the brain and, individually, serve integrating functions related to a variety of sensory inputs. Each association area of cortex coordinates the functioning of nearby sensory areas. For example, visual cortex is located in the rear of the cerebral cortex in both hemispheres. Damage to these areas results in reduced vision or even blindness. But near visual cortex is a large area of cortex related in a different way to visual experience. The visual association area lies lateral to visual cortex all the way to the posterior edges of the temporal and parietal lobes. This area is involved in visual recognition and comprehension. There are also similar integrative areas in each hemisphere for touch and auditory (hearing) functions. Damage to auditory association cortex will not affect an animal's ability to distinguish between two tones of different frequency (agnosia). What the animal can no longer do is distinguish between two series of tones. The problem is not sensory but one of integration.

Injuries to the parietal lobe of the brain can produce a variety of impairments. A person may not be able to recognize an object in the hand by touch alone. A person may completely neglect one side of the body. Familiar faces may not be recognized. Spatial orientation may be disturbed. These widely diverse types of impairment arise from parietal-lobe injuries, because the lobe is positioned adjacent to visual, auditory, and sensory regions. Lesions at the anterior end of the parietal region produce contralateral sensory deficits that involve complex sensory information. For example, after injury in the parietal cortex of the right hemisphere, a key placed in the left hand and manipulated cannot be identified as a key. In astereognosis, as this deficit is labeled, the subject feels an object in his hand but cannot identify it.

There are also association-cortex deficits known as apraxias. These involve motor functioning in which the person can no longer connect current perceptions with the memories of objects and their functions. "Dressing apraxia," for example, leaves one with a strange problem. The person seems normal in conversation and movements, but when he picks up a jacket, he cannot put it on. He is unable to sequence the right behaviors with the right parts of the jacket and the body.

In general, the apraxias and agnosias cannot be reliably located in strict regions of the parietal lobe. The exact location for different problems seems different for each person. Interestingly, more agnosias and apraxias occur in injuries to the dominant hemisphere (usually the left).

These association-cortex deficits seem to suggest that in normal human functioning there is need for a close association between long-term memories and current sensory experiences. As mentioned in chapter 1, there are related difficulties with regard to facial recognition. A man who can see normally may fail to recognize his wife or pictures of her. Apparently, current perceptions cannot be compared to stored memories. Damage to the brain in these ways leaves a person floundering for meaning to stimuli, since he cannot connect the stimuli to interpretive contexts. Life becomes a maze of unidentifiable stimuli. This is similar to what seems to happen to a person suffering from total amnesia. A woman, for example, does not know her own name, cannot recognize familiar people, and recalls nothing about her former career or family. She is perfectly normal, though, in her ability to learn new things. The problem once again is one of matching permanent memories to current experience. Upon receiving information about her life, such an amnesiac learns the facts as if they referred to another person. To hear about her spouse and family is for her to be learning about some other person. The amnesiac cannot tie all of these facts to herself, to her personal history. The very stuff of self-awareness seems to depend, in part, on association-cortex functions, which tie complex sensations of the present with a personal record from the past, creating the feelings of personhood in the form of a connected stream of consciousness. There are individuals who, through some sort of brain damage, have lost the ability to form new long-term memories. Short-term memories last, for the most part, just several minutes. If they are not coded into long-term memory storage, they are permanently lost. After a person has lost the ability to move memories from short term to the permanent long term, he or she loses a portion of personal awareness. After an accident a man may be told he was in the accident, where he is, and so on. But in a few minutes he may forget and ask again about what happened to him. He cannot begin a magazine article and finish it if it is too long, because he forgets the first part of the article before he gets to the end. In such a case, his personal life becomes increasingly tragic. Since he has retrained all his old memories up to the date of the accident, he can live without problems at home, as long as it is in the same house as before the accident. If he moves to another city, he is forever lost. It is always a strange house and neighborhood. His children grow up and change appearance and thus become more like strangers than family. Life becomes a tragedy of a depersonalized present-tense experience. With the absence of long-term memory, he fails to make the association needed for daily living and a continuing personal experience.

It is likely that animals with little or no association cortex (which includes most animals) must experience, in large part, a present-tense life with no self-awareness. Though I can only speculate, life must resemble for these animals some of our own dreams, although perhaps with more order and dependability. In dream states we have no awareness of the dream as a dream until we begin to wake up. We simply move as a part of the dream from one event to the next. Time does not flow dependably; personalities, including our own, change spontaneously; stories change in mid-course. And none of this bothers us, because we are not there as ourselves. We are the dream. If this is what most animals experience—in the absence of the ability to associate large areas of their experiences together into meaningful wholes and lacking language to label any holistic experiences—they must be controlled solely by environmental stimuli, just as the famous empiricist B. F. Skinner claims. Most animals would be determined by their environments, because they cannot construct a continuing self that has existence apart from a particular momentary configuration of stimuli.

In animals such as the apes, which have larger areas of association cortex, it is reasonable to suggest that these cortical areas aid the animal in learning tasks, which involves connecting memories to new stimuli and discerning sequences and alterations of stimuli. In the absence of inherited instincts, these animals are designed to constantly stretch their experience backwards and forwards over short periods of time. But they show nothing in their behavior, or in behavioral deficits after brain damage to association areas of cortex, that would suggest the degree of awareness possessed by humans. There may exist long-term holistic experiences in the mind of the chimpanzee or gorilla, but nothing in their behavior indicates that these experiences ever form more than a glimmer of one's self as going through the experiences. Nothing in the chimpanzee's behavior indicates that it is able to speculate on the meaning of its experiences, a process that requires far more sophistication in the synthesizing of personal and shared experiences.

The human being, on the other hand, contemplates the mystery of his or her continuing existence and the meaning of that existence. Meaning begins with the ability to integrate facts and events into a whole. The human personality is an integrated element supported by legions of neural networks in the association cortex. Eastern mystics try to gain meaning in this vast sensory world by cancelling sensory input through meditation, until in the absence of sensory data the self-experience dissolves and they become "one" with the universe. All experience is then apparently unified, with no disarray, into the sum total of all meaning. Unfortunately, the personality has been lost, integrated back into nothingness. Western-world people have generally believed that by connecting sensory inputs into progressively larger wholes (formulae, stories, art), we gain meaning. Total meaning must elude us, though, since not one of us can connect all things together. However, the body human, with its complex association cortex, does prepare us to move along toward meaning. Without association cortex, I would strain my mind to recall what this pen is doing in my hand—and whose hand is it, anyway?— let alone write something with meaning. Human beings, with their massive association cortex, are able to connect the experiences of life together and relate them to self for a greater experience of the world and personal awareness. Sense and memory are combined and soon join reason, language, and larger experiences. Then, just like a microscope put into focus, the universe becomes visible.

Hemisphere Specialization

Another uniqueness of the body human is that our brains are not completely symmetrical with regard to the functions of the two halves. We have hemispheric specializations that make us completely unique in the animal

world. Humans have some functions that are more involved with one side of the brain than the other, even
though the two hemispheres have much in common. The
two hemispheres are connected by the large corpus callosum (and two smaller commissures), which is made of
several hundred million neural fibers that coordinate and
exchange information between the hemispheres. The corpus callosum is relatively larger in man than in any animal, suggesting that the integration of the different kinds
of information from each hemisphere is important.

The concept of hemisphere specialization is most easily seen in the existence of a speech center in the brain.
Speech is almost always controlled by the left side of the
brain, whether a person is left- or right-handed. A dra-
matic demonstration of the presence of speech capabilities in only one hemisphere is provided by the Wada Test.
In this test, the drug sodium amytal, a barbiturate chemi-
cally similar to the ingredients in sleeping pills, is injected
into the right carotid artery. The fully conscious patient
has arms raised in the air and is counting when the drug is
injected. Within seconds the left arm falls limp. This indicates that the drug has reached the right hemisphere,
which controls the left side of the body, and it has taken
its deadening effect. The patient, though, continues counting. If the drug had been injected so that it reached the
left hemisphere, the patient would have gone speechless
for several minutes, depending on the drug dosage. Only
rarely would one discover a person who had speech controlled by the right hemisphere.

The exact relationship between the left-hemispheric
speech center and a handedness preference in humans is
not well understood. It is known that in all cultures most
human beings, perhaps as high as 90 percent, are right-
handed. The small percentage of left-handers may have

led to some of our negative, prejudiced terms, such as a "left-handed compliment." Right-handed preference seems to have existed far back into history. Subjects in cave paintings are usually holding weapons in their right hands. Stone-age tools are usually shaped to fit the right hand. Skull fractures from the bones of animals preyed upon by humans long ago show that most fractures of the skull are on the animal's left side. This suggests that the attacker struck the blow with an implement held in the right hand. Tracings of the hand made by Cro-Magnon people show over 80 percent to be of the left hand, meaning that the right hand made the tracing. Interestingly, when some of these artists wished to paint hand outlines, they sometimes used an early form of spray painting. They apparently filled their mouth with paint and blew it around the hand. It certainly would not have been hard to spot an artist in those days. The red mouth would have given him away.

Animals may show preferences for using the right or left paw in certain situations, but they divide up fairly evenly into right- and left-handers. It is impossible to breed handedness in animals. Therefore, any preference is not genetic, but reflects chance learning by the animal. Anatomical asymmetries of the brain are not found in any animals with the exception of the chimpanzee and the gorilla, where the structural difference between right and left hemispheres is slight. There is also no indication that such differences relate to language abilities in chimps. Songbirds, however, do show some hemispheric specialization with regard to vocal control and sound production. Some birds are highly similar to human beings in their voice-production machinery. The voice organ of the bird consists of the syrinx, an air-driven structure that produces sound. Thin membranes in this organ are controlled

by adjacent muscles innervated by the right and left hypoglossal nerves. These are cranial nerves controlling the
musculature of the neck. Sectioning only a songbird's left
hypoglossal nerve destroys the structure of any bird songs
or silences the bird, whereas sectioning the right hypoglossal nerve produces barely any change in the bird's
singing. This shows a left-hemisphere dominance of vocal-
control mechanisms in these birds. These asymmetries in
control of bird songs appear to extend to the highest brain
areas controlling song. Lesions of the left hemisphere
completely destroy song structure, and singing becomes
unstable and monotonous. Minimal effects follow right-
hemisphere lesions. In these left-hemisphere–damaged
birds, some singing recovers as the right hemisphere takes
over function.

The specializations of the right and left hemispheres in
the human brain have been best illustrated in recent years
by the split-brain operation, designed to provide relief
from frequent and disabling epileptic seizures. Since the
hemispheres routinely share information with each other,
epileptic activity in one hemisphere quickly spreads to the
other. Surgically cutting the corpus callosum serves to
greatly reduce the frequency and severity of the patient's
seizures. With the hemispheres severed, an experimenter
can selectively send information to either hemisphere and
thus test the capabilities of each side of the brain.

Results of split-brain experiments have shown that only
the activity occurring in the left hemisphere could be
described verbally by the patients. When a patient holds
an apple in his right hand (controlled by the left hemisphere), he is able to say what he is holding even though he
cannot see it. However, when the apple is held in the left
hand (controlled by the right hemisphere), the patient
whose speech is controlled by the left hemisphere does not

report holding anything. The left "speaking" brain has no information about the right-brain–controlled left hand.

This separation of left and right hemispheres of the brain has allowed researchers to test each half independently to discern its special abilities. Speech is contained in the left hemisphere and is either totally absent or greatly reduced in the right hemisphere. However, the right hemisphere will work with spatial and, to some degree, numerical information. The right hemisphere, for example, is superior to the left hemisphere at arranging blocks to match a sample pattern. Even though I am right-handed, my right hemisphere and left hand would be able to draw a better cube than my left hemisphere and right hand (assuming I had a split brain, of course). Apparently, our artistic skills with our right hands are due chiefly to the sharing of right-hemisphere abilities with the left hemisphere.

The left hemisphere is superior at analytic skills, of which language is the outstanding example. More speculative ideas, particularly from psychologist Robert Ornstein, suggest that the left hemisphere is more rational and analytical, whereas the right hemisphere is more intuitive and holistic in operation.[3]

The question naturally arises as to why the human brain possesses some rather sharp distinctions between left and right hemispheric functions. Why are speech abilities, for example, not simply duplicated in both left and right hemispheres and thus protected against damage to one of the hemispheres? Considering songbirds, which also possess left-hemispheric control of complex vocalization, it may be true that duplication of the system controlling the intricacies of speech would use up too much valuable cortical

3. Robert Ornstein, *The Psychology of Consciousness* (New York: Harcourt Brace Jovanovich, Inc., 1977).

material. The often-quoted saying that we use only 20 percent of our brain has been circulated in the past because
we did not know what 80 percent of the brain did. But 80
percent of the brain is not electrically inactive. To use
more cortical matter for a second speech system might tax
other systems too greatly. This might also be true of the
songbird's small brain.

But it is also true that our right hemisphere seems to
possess abilities complementary to the left, suggesting
perhaps that each hemisphere engages in a separate way
of analyzing and synthesizing data to create human experience. These two separate perspectives on reality contained within one brain could then be integrated together
to form a greatly enhanced experience and response to reality. Human knowledge may be a product of the left hemisphere's cortical analysis of experience (with the symbols
of language), and the right hemisphere's patterning of that
data into some meaningful whole. Effective thinking and
experiential living as a human being seem to require both
rational and intuitive ingredients. This is reflected in our
attempts to give priority to both the sciences and the arts
in our liberal-arts institutions.

Perhaps the reason that these two distinct ways of
knowing have been partially separated into the two hemispheres of the brain is to allow each to process information without excessive interference by the other. The
separation of the two modes of processing information
places limits on hemispheric dominance, perhaps in order
that the language-dominant hemisphere does not eliminate right-hemispheric processing. The same situation
allows for the possibility of individual differences with regard to the blend of rational and intuitive thinking. Individual differences in right- and left-hemisphere interaction are seen between the two sexes. For example, the
right hemisphere is known to develop faster in boys than

the left. In girls the reverse is true. Considerable evidence suggests that females are superior to males in a wide range of skills that require the use of language. Males are known to be superior in tasks that are spatial in nature.[4]

Each person's experience is enriched by inputs from both hemispheres. Each couple or family is blessed by the differences between male and female thinking. Each culture owes a debt to an entire continuum of people, ranging from the very rational to the very artistic.

Animals with no lateralization of brain functions can have none of the advantages in thinking and experience that combining rational and intuitive modes of processing can offer. Great ideas and constructions, in both science and art, must proceed with both sides of the ladder of knowing, each assisting the other. Animal experiences cannot reverberate these two epistemologies back and forth in the brain. Nor does the animal brain possess the dominating characteristic of language, which the body human bestows on the left hemisphere. Language provides the symbolic frames for merging reason and holistic experience into thought.

Speech Center

Undoubtedly, the most unique part of the human brain is the speech center. In the late nineteenth century, neurologist Paul Broca discovered that lesions in the left hemisphere produced language impairments. This speech region is responsible for a person's ability to acquire any language by being exposed to it. It also initiates control of the subtle changes in throat and mouth musculature according to memories and simultaneous feedback of a person's own words. Such a speech center has never been discovered in any animal—and, indeed, no animal

4. Sally P. Springer and Georg Deutsch, *Left Brain Right Brain* (San Francisco: W. H. Freeman and Co., 1981).

possesses man's language capabilities. Brain stimulation of animal cerebral cortex generally fails to elicit any vocalization at all. Since animal vocalizations are more involved in flight, defense, attack, feeding, and sexual behavior, it is understandable that electrical stimulation of the limbic system and related structures within the brain is more likely to produce vocalizations. On the other hand, removing parts of the cerebral cortex of primates has little effect on their vocalization. It is clear that there are no similar speech centers in animals.

Without the evidence of gradual approximations of the human speech center in the animal world, the development of human speech from the animals is a mystery to biologists. Though weak, the best explanations are that gestures were replaced by single sounds or that men began to imitate sounds in their natural environment. The complexity of all human languages (past and present), the neurological complexity required to produce grammatical knowledge in the child, and the complexity of neurological control over auditory and musculature systems required for speech make these explanations appear absurd. If we are honest, we will face the facts and admit that we can find no evolutionary development to explain our unique speech center.

A lot of our understanding of the mechanisms of the speech center comes from the observations of language impairment following left-hemisphere brain damage. Whenever people suffer the loss of language functions through such damage, they are tragically cut off from the worlds of meaning and personal communication. Disorders of language due to brain damage are called aphasias. The particular symptoms of aphasias depend on the location of the injury within the speech center. Damage to Broca's area, in the frontal-lobe portion of the speech center, is appropriately called Broca's aphasia. Such patients have difficulty in speech production and cannot produce the words to say what they want to say. Speech is quite slow and labored or, most often, not present at all. These patients can usually write words and can understand written and spoken words. Electrical stimulation of Broca's area has been shown to arrest ongoing speech. It may be assumed that Broca's aphasia destroys an executive control system for speech. The output of Broca's area must reach the nearby motor cortical areas involved in activating the appropriate musculature in the face and throat. Apparently, in Broca's aphasia, the lips are ready to speak, but—to the frustration of the patient—the words just will not come out. The only effortless words that this patient can utter are curses, as if a separate cursing mechanism exists.

In another injury, Wernicke's aphasia, damage is posterior to Broca's area, in the temporal-parietal cortex. In this aphasia there is a deficit in language comprehension. Unlike Broca's aphasia, speech in this case is effortless and fluent, but it does not make any sense. It is just a lot of gibberish and meaningless arrangements of words. Both speech and writing are equally affected, and these patients often have no comprehension of language. Apparently, the memories of the sounds of words are stored in Wernicke's area, which allows us to recognize words, as opposed to Broca's area, which allows us to produce words.

The tragedy of these aphasias to the human person is great. If we had such damage, we would be able to think clearly but would be unable to say anything meaningful. People would look at us with puzzled gazes. Our own words might sound like gibberish to us, making us feel mentally ill. We would be distant from normal human contact. Other limited forms of aphasia exist. In alexia, the person cannot read any longer. In agraphia, a person cannot write. In anomia, objects cannot be named. In conduction aphasia, the patient cannot repeat words. In the strange mixed-transcortical aphasia, speech and comprehension are destroyed, yet the person can repeat strings of words. There are alexics who can read numbers, even Roman numerals, but not letters and words.

To lose language is to lose contact with others and become trapped in a shell of frustration. But a functioning speech center places at our command verbal symbols as tools to give a symbolic picture of the meaning and unity emerging from our perceptions, feelings, and thoughts.

The Essence of Personhood

We have been looking at the major neurological systems that distinguish our brain from that of all subhuman animals. Without even considering the broader mysteries of matter and mind, it is clear that the body human has been designed for the mental state of personhood. The speech center, the association cortex, the frontal lobes, and the hemispheric specialization characterize the very nature of the human brain. How these major systems came to exist in the human brain is a question that has not yielded to merely biological explanations.

The unique purposes of these brain distinctions for the body human are enormous. They give meaning to the array of sensory input—through association, through symbolic labels of language, and through left- and right-hemispheric differences. We are able to operate in a world of meaning, contacting other persons, sharing experiences and knowledge, building the heritage of culture, and standing on memories, while reaching toward plans, goals, and aspirations unique to human nature. The brain of the body human makes all this possible.

Jim Whitmer

7 Till Death Do Us In

Man outlives every creature on the planet ... except trees and an occasional tortoise.

There is a tragic disease in some children in which aging seems to be accelerated. These children seem to age ten years for every one of ours, so that a balding, wrinkled child of ten soon dies of old age. Such a child's life appears to be but a segment of time-lapse photography. Any adult who watches the disease progress can visualize more clearly what is occurring in all of us though a fraction more slowly. The disease is called infantile progeria, or Hutchinson-Gilford syndrome, and the symptoms usually begin to manifest themselves before the child's first birthday. While other children's brand-new bodies are beginning to walk and run and discover new sights and smells, the progeria victim's body is aging. The progeria child's growth is retarded and severe dwarfing sets in, giving the hapless child an abnormal appearance. Even though these children do not mature sexually, their disease gives them all the appearances of getting old. Their hair is lost early and their skin appears aged. They develop severe atherosclerosis in all their major blood vessels as early as nine years old. The ten-year-old looks seventy and usually such a child dies at a very young chronological age.

It is difficult for the rest of us, who think of life as at

least seventy years, to accept progeria in a child. To compress life into a single decade seems so unfair. More time is needed to see what the world offers, to reflect on things great and small, to marry, to see grandchildren, to relax in the cool evening breeze. But even three-score-and-ten is not enough time to do all that we must do, when, as the Preacher wrote so long ago in Ecclesiastes, "Thou hast placed eternity in our hearts." Seventy years may seem like an eternity to a child, but not to the sixty-five-year-old retiree. To die of a heart attack at forty-two, or lung cancer at twenty-nine, or in an automobile accident at seventeen, seems especially unfair, because the needed years have been so deplorably stolen away.

Moses once wrote of men living to great ages, greater than nine hundred years. Methuselah lives on in our world as a symbol of old age because he lived nine hundred sixty and nine years before he died in the year the great flood began. If Adam, who lived to be nine hundred and thirty years, would appear today and observe that most humans age and die by their seventies, he would stare in disbelief and sorrow, just as we stare at the progeria victim. What for us is so natural—to live to our seventies and beyond—to Adam would be a travesty of the natural. To be scarcely mature and yet die would seem absurd. I assume that a race of all progeria victims would think nothing unnatural about living only one decade and then dying of old age—except that they would share the same longing for eternity and the time to fulfill their human potential that we have.

If seventy years or perhaps longer seems condensed to us, and its brevity threatens the meaning of daily life, then it is helpful to see our life-span relative to other creatures with which we share the planet. Our pet dog is senile at eighteen, young to us but very old for a dog. Rats will live only four to five years. The tiny shrew's whole life spans eighteen months. He races around as if he knows his time is short. A male black widow spider averages only a hundred days, a summer and then some. Some butterflies live just over forty days. The male housefly manages to live only nine days. I have sometimes wondered where all those flies that sneak into the house ahead of me went. Each one that entered had a funeral in a little over a week. The mayfly passes its whole life as an adult in just several hours. Life is so short for a mayfly that it doesn't even have a mouth for eating. How can one find meaning and purpose in just three hours? It is a good thing that mayflies cannot think, or too bad, perhaps, that *we* can.

But perhaps there is some mercy in this parade of short-lived insects and animals. We outlive them all. Our maximum life-span appears to be about a hundred and twenty years, though few of us live that long. In fact, we outlive every creature on the globe, except trees and an occasional tortoise. But our long life is a mystery. The usual biological indications for long life in an animal do not apply to us. We simply live much too long by those standards. We are not exceptionally large, nor do we possess a comparatively low metabolic rate. We are also not especially healthy. We are often sick, are prone to disease, and have a deleterious gene pool, forever surfacing in one deformity after another.

Aging itself is a mystery. On the biological level, we do not really know what causes aging. There are theories, of course, but no one is convinced that the answer has been found. The aging process and all the negative consequences it brings to the body and lifestyle are understandably a concern of ours, because we live so long. With a longer life we get to see and feel more acutely the changes that occur in an aging body. Pain strikes a knee when we are six because we fell while racing down the stairs. When we are in our teens we hurt a knee playing tennis. In our fifties knee problems flare up continually as we jog. In our seventies our daily experience is often one of painful arthritis in each knee. The body is wearing out continuously and will eventually die when disease or malfunction destroys some critical body organ.

Increasing pain with age and our awareness of the approach of death place us in an existential crisis. When we reflect on the certainty of death, we ask more questions about the meaning and purpose of life. Does anything really matter, when the universe will eventually rub out any trace of our ever having existed? What purpose could the increasing amount of pain and suffering serve, if death ends it all? Those are the questions that the body human gives the mind time to reflect on as it searches for answers. The only other possibility is to have a life so short that there is no time for pain or for finding meaning in that pain. We could have been designed like a mayfly, with no mind to speak of, and only hours to live. There would be little time for pain, no awareness of it anyway, and little to do but breed and die. This is "success" to nature, but then the mayfly in nature seems to be merely a complicated gene carrier. The body human's design says that the essence of human nature is more and that we need time to find the meaning of our existence.

The Length of Life—Of Mice and Men

Many individuals live to be over a hundred years old. No mouse lives more than four years. It is strange that two mammals that are similar in so many ways should have such different life-spans. What is more amazing is that the human body is not the best-designed body for surviving in nature's battles. We do not have the tremendous strength of an elephant, the speed of a horse, or the swimming ability of a seal. We have no camouflage, no claws, no armor, and no wings. A human is actually a very sickly and weak creature. Why, then, do we live so long? Actually, we do not know why. Furthermore, the advantage of a long life after the child-rearing years, when an animal weakens, does not seem to fit in with nature's program of "survival of the fittest."

The oldest man in the world until recently was Shigechiyo Izumi of Japan, who turned 120 on June 29, 1985. He died before he had another birthday. Until his death he held the *Guinness Book of World Records* title as the world's oldest person. He is, therefore, a good example to illustrate the potential life-span of man. As Shigechiyo Izumi showed, it seems we have about a 120-year maximum life-span. Even though most of us will never see our 120th birthday, it is obvious that we have the potential for a much longer life than nearly every animal.

The length of our life-span draws attention to the unusual menopausal state of human females, which begins twenty to thirty years before she dies. Monkeys and apes continue to menstruate after their reproductive period and usually show no menopause. It seems as if the human female (and male) are given many years of life *after* raising their family, while most animals die shortly after their child-bearing and -rearing usefulness is gone. This makes sense if we have more purpose in life than just to reproduce a replacement for ourselves. Man is not merely the genes' way of making other genes. We are persons and, after the important task of raising the family, still have many years to experience life.

Humans are outlived considerably by trees, but it is

hard to compare our life-span to that of trees, because trees seem practically immortal. Pulitzer Prize-winning Annie Dillard reverently described the long-living trees:

> Trees do not accumulate life, but deadwood, like a thickening coat of mail. Their odds actually improve as they age. Some trees, like giant Sequoias, are, practically speaking, immortal, vulnerable only to another ice age. They are not even susceptible to fire. Sequoia wood barely burns, and the bark is nearly as fireproof as asbestos. The top of one Sequoia, struck by lightning a few years ago during a July thunderstorm, smouldered quietly, without apparently damaging the tree, until it was put out by a snowstorm in October. Some trees sink taproots to rock. Some spread wide mats of roots clutching at acres. They will not be blown. We run around these obelisk creatures teetering on our soft, small feet. We are out on a jaunt, picnicking, fattening like puppies for our deaths. Shall I carve a name on this trunk? What if I fell in a forest? Would a tree hear?[1]

The unusualness of our life-span becomes more obvious when we compare it with a sampling of some other of earth's creatures. The following are all maximal life-spans, usually observed in animals in captivity. As with human beings, very few of these animals or insects ever reach their maximal age, because of the rigors of life and survival. On the brief end of the spectrum of life, the rotifer, depending on the species, will have a life of several days to several months. Butterflies may live only six weeks. The male black widow spider may live 100 days, the female 271 days. Life-span in the honeybee is short, but it will vary, depending on the needs of the colony. In temperate zones the colony is inhabited by two types of bees, summer and winter bees. They represent two different

1. Annie Dillard, *Pilgrim at Tinker Creek* (New York: Bantam Books, 1975) pp. 93–94.

generations of bees. The summer bee is to be found in the colony between May and August. Its average life-span varies from 25–35 days, with a maximum of 60–70 days. Difficulties of surviving the winter are overcome in the honeybee by the colony's production in the autumn of a long-lived generation with more body reserves. The winter bee will live about six or seven months, until spring.

Some beetles manage to live eleven years and the length of life of the seventeen-year cicada is no secret. One of the tapeworms, which lives in human beings, has a life-span of thirty-five years. While the great majority of insects probably live less than one year, the record holder is probably the queen termite, who may lay eggs for fifty years! Actually, the longer life of the queen termite guarantees her no more meaning in life than the several hours of the mayfly.

In the vertebrates the life-spans are just as variable as the invertebrates. The following chart lists the maximal ages of common animals, in years.[2]

Capuchin monkey	40	Aardvark	12
Rhesus monkey	29	Seal	34
Squirrel monkey	21	Dog	20
Chimpanzee	44	Cat	28
Gorilla	54	Brown bear	36
Goat	18	Whale	80
Domestic cattle	30	Porcupine	27
Swine	27	Guinea pig	7
Sheep	20	Mink	10
Camel	29	African fruit bat	21
Horse	46	Hedgehog	4
Rhinoceros	40	Shrew	1½
Indian elephant	70	Platypus	17

2. Adapted from Marion J. Lamb, *Biology of Aging* (New York: John Wiley and Sons, 1977) p. 46, and Caleb E. Finch and Leonard Hayflick (eds.), *Handbook of the Biology of Aging* (New York: VanNostrand Reinhold Co., 1977) p. 9.

The Cause of Longevity

Size/Metabolic Rate

In general, the best predictors of life-span in the animal world are size and metabolic rate. Basically, larger animals have slower metabolic rates and tend to live longer than smaller animals. Probably their internal organs simply do not have to work as hard and therefore last longer. The smallest mammal, the fierce little shrew, which is smaller than a mouse, lives for only eighteen months, whereas the elephant and the whale manage about seventy years. The metabolic rate of the shrew is so high (heartbeat of 1200/minute) that the shrew literally vibrates as it frets around looking for food. Due to its small size and heat-loss problems, it must eat continually or die. The elephant, at the other extreme, has a heartbeat of 30/minute and usually moves with a determined slowness. A measurement of the white whale's heartbeat shows it to be 16–17/minute. In between these extremes, metabolism slows as animal size increases. The mouse has a heartbeat of 650/minute, the cat 150/minute, the horse 40/minute.

Human beings, however, do not fit this pattern. We are not even close to the pattern. We are about the size of a chimpanzee and have a heart rate of about seventy per minute, and yet we live three times as long as a chimp. While body size and metabolic rate are not perfect predictors of the life-span of animals, they are generally quite accurate. There are exceptions to these predictions, however, none is as outstanding as the body human.

Prolificacy

Among mammals of similar size, the most prolific species are very often the shortest-lived. The shrew's litter size is often five to ten, and the female usually raises two litters a year, dying at the end of her first breeding season. However, small bats living in the same environment are less prolific but have longer lives. To the great horseshoe bat of Western Europe only one young bat is born each year, yet the potential life-span of this species exceeds fifteen years in the wild. While high fecundity is probably not directly responsible for shorter life-spans, there does appear to be in mammals a good correlation between the two.

Genetic Factors

There is also some evidence of a correlation between the life-spans of parents and children, but it is difficult to know without more studies whether there is a genetic or environmental reason for this. Also suggesting a genetic link in longevity is the observation that in most animals the male sex is shorter-lived. This is true in creatures as dissimilar as fish, spiders, houseflies, and man. There are exceptions to this rule among mammals, however, such as the stallion and the male Syrian hamster.

Size of the Brain

Brain size also relates to potential longevity and may explain man's great longevity. Many large-brained animals live longer than smaller-brained animals of equal body size. This theory would suggest that a larger brain is an advantage to life because it participates in the stabilization of the life processes. The brain controls the physiological, biochemical, and behavioral performances that relate to long life, especially in the use of superior homeostatic regulatory mechanisms.

We have not yet found any convincing theory that explains the longevity of human beings. By a wide margin, man is longer-lived than any of the primates and, by a smaller margin, any of the mammals. We may not outlive certain trees and a few tortoises, but their extended life-spans come at great cost. Trees buy longer life at the price of passivity. Tortoises who have occasionally lived up to a hundred and fifty years are pictures of cold-blooded slow motion. Humans, on the other hand, are hot-blooded creatures of activity. How and why we live so long remains a mystery.

The Signs of Aging

Our longevity gives us the opportunity to study and experience the phenomena of aging and the inevitable decline of the human body. Much more of this decline is noticeable today, since medical advances make it possible to prolong the life of many individuals who would in previous times have normally succumbed to disease at an earlier age. Aging symptoms—wrinkled skin, gray hair, and weaker muscles—are basically manifestations of an underlying failure in cell efficiency, which affects every organ system of the body. Cell failure is apparently a picture of some deeper disturbances in the molecular world. These same changes during old age portray what has essentially been occurring since birth: the passage toward death.[3]

One of the most common signs of aging is a graying of the hair, which usually begins about age thirty. Although most mammals show little or no change in hair pigmentation with age, a few domesticated species, such as the dog, the sheep, and the horse, show graying with advancing age. In addition, in humans the skin wrinkles and grows less

3. Lamb, *Biology of Ageing,* p. 54.

pliable, and there is a general loss of physical strength. After the age of forty, there are deteriorations in blood pressure, the capacity of the lungs, hearing, eyesight, manual dexterity, and mental reaction time. There is also a decline in the effectiveness of the homeostatic regulatory mechanisms. The greatest negative changes in the body occur to those functions that involve coordinated activity of a number of organ systems. Single organs and their related systems show much less change with aging. For example, human nerve-conduction velocity declines by 10 percent between the ages of twenty and ninety, whereas the maximum breathing capacity declines by 50 percent. The former is a measurement of the performance of only the nerves. The latter depends on the efficiency and coordination of both the nervous and the muscular systems. With aging, humans may also lose up to an inch of height, and there is also a slight decrease in the size of the extremities of the body. (The ears, however, become larger with age, and there is a thickening of the earlobe.)

Bones and joints show characteristic changes with aging. The knee joint, being a complicated structure, is a good example of the early onset of aging. By the fourth decade of life, changes due to aging are found in the knees of both sexes. The patella (kneecap) begins to show irregularities, with thin shreds of superficial cartilage partially detached and slight degenerative changes in the adjacent leg bones.

At least in Western societies, the process of aging is also marked by fat accumulation in both males and females, to the point that aging is almost synonymous with "putting on the pounds." Both sexes show increasing accumulation of fat deposits around the pelvic girdle, with females more likely to gain around the hips and upper thighs.

Wrinkling of the skin is a predictable product of

aging, but it is markedly increased by exposure to sunlight. Slight facial wrinkling may begin as early as twenty, and wrinkling is generally use-related. Facial wrinkling therefore centers around the areas utilized by constant frowning and smiling. But some wrinkling is clearly not use-related, as in the case of the earlobe, which seems puffy and enlarged by the sixth decade and shows variable wrinkling. In the very old, fine wrinkling covers the arms and face in ways unrelated to the distribution of the facial muscles. This wrinkling has a crisscross-patterned appearance, much like crumpled paper.

In addition to the graying already mentioned, with age comes hair loss. Since hair loss is genetic and related to androgen (male hormone) production, it affects men more than women. All body hairs, including pubic hair, become less numerous with aging, and the very old have comparatively little body hair.

Brain-cell loss occurs with aging, causing a 7 percent decrease in brain matter by the age of eighty. This percentage loss of neurons in the brain is not necessarily detrimental to the mental and physical activities of the elderly. The speed of axonal conduction in the brain is unchanged with normal aging, but synaptic transmission from one neuron to the next appears to be retarded. This may be responsible for the slower reaction time and alpha wave of the elderly.

Of all the bodily changes in the aging process, it is the aging of the cardiovascular system that is central to the entire phenomenon. A declining cardiovascular system may be partly responsible for the general physiological decline of the aged. It is well known that the major causes of death in an aging population are diseases of the cardiovascular system. With passing years, blood-circulation time increases, and there is a decline in the system's ability to transport oxygen. Consequently, thermoregulation, which depends in large measure on heat conductance by cutaneous blood flow, becomes less efficient with age. With each passing year, there is a decrease in the ability of the heart to contract, an increased stiffness of the large arteries, and an increase in peripheral resistance. Probably all human beings show increased atherosclerosis (a term interchangeable with arteriosclerosis in common usage) with aging, although its severity varies with different individuals. Overeating (particularly of animal fats) and a stressful lifestyle increase the risk factor for cardiovascular disease in most individuals.

The cardiovascular system has not been designed to last forever. While many body organs are composed of cells that are constantly replacing themselves, the cardiovascular system is composed of post-mitotic cells that cannot divide and are thus present for the life of the individual. This is also true of skeletal muscle and nervous tissue in the brain and spinal cord. The stable cells of these areas undergo increased morphological and chemical alterations with age. It is obvious that not only will the aging body have weakened muscles, but also that two very important organs, the heart and brain, which support or organize so many other body functions, are going to be increasingly responsible for deficiencies in the entire human body.

Theories of Aging

All theories about why we grow old relate to the different types of matter in the body human. Our bodies are composed of cells that multiply throughout life (white corpuscles, epithelial cells), cells that are incapable of division (neurons, heart-muscle cells), and noncellular material that may have much or little turnover (intercellular substance). Some theories of aging say that the body declines through mutational or immunological changes in the properties of the cells. Other theories relate aging to the loss of or injury to nonmultiplying cells. Finally, there are theories that look at the changes in the inert materials of the body as producing aging symptoms.

It is clear to see how damage and deterioration to the nonrenewable neurons of the brain could contribute increasingly to the disabilities associated with aging in the human body. Something similar may also be occurring in renewable systems as well. It has been shown that cells derived from human fetal tissues are not capable of being propagated indefinitely but are capable of making only about fifty divisions. Why these cells are limited with regard to multiplication is not known. By contrast, in the amoeba or in bacteria, limitless division is possible. Yet fifty divisions in human cells may be sufficient to supply

Josephine Berger at age 20 and 90.

all the body's needs—or they may not be. In the latter case, deterioration would be found in those organs because of lack of cell replacement. If cell division continued in those cells or was present in brain or heart cells, human life might be extended by hundreds of years without degenerative symptoms of aging such as declining vigor, susceptibility to disease, wrinkled skin, and so on. Perhaps the Genesis accounts of the antediluvian world are an accurate remembrance of a time when life-spans were considerably longer.

It is possible that aging begins at the molecular level, where accidents are inevitable. DNA bases may be damaged, and errors can be made in the translation of genetic information. As a result of such molecular defects, subcellular problems such as enzyme defects may arise. Accumulated flaws would affect the cellular environment, resulting in cell death or cell deficiencies. These cellular problems would soon contaminate tissues and organs, and the whole organism would degenerate and progress toward death.

Whatever the cause, aging and death, like taxes, are inevitable. It almost forces one to conclude that something has gone wrong with nature. Life has been given limits. Human life has been confined within narrow boundaries of time. But the body human helps by giving us more time than animals and mammals before the inevitable decay and death. Things could be worse. We could be mayflies, with only several hours to contemplate the meaning of life.

The Problem of Pain and Death

Childbirth causes pain in only one creature on earth, the human female. This is partly a consequence of the relatively large cranium of the human infant. It seems appropriate that this is a uniquely human pain, since human beings experience more pain and suffering than any other creature on earth. The body human is exquisitely tuned to experience the world, pain as well as pleasure. In addition, all of our pain or pleasure is filtered through the mind to be magnified or minimized. Since the human mind can fear the coming pain or anticipate other negative consequences, the pain is thus doubled. The human being experiences more pain and for a longer length of life than any animal. In addition, the pains endured by the human being are not just physical. If only they were, then we might be able to bear them without objecting. Pain becomes "suffering" when it exists predominantly in the mind. A child dies and the parents suffer. A suitor is rejected and he suffers. A child with cerebral palsy is ridiculed at school and she suffers, and her parents suffer. A man abuses his children and then cries in guilt, and the whole family suffers. A president dies and the whole nation suffers.

Are we fortunate beings or not? The body human is finely tuned to sense reality with a mind-brain capable of interpretation and distortion, and so we feel more pain. The human being is a person, open to all the joys of personhood but also the sufferings of personhood. The animal world is excused from the agonies of personhood. Buffaloes do not worry about their looks or their ultimate death. It serves no purpose for the buffalo. But what purpose could it serve for persons? As we have seen, the body human is specially designed to develop personhood in human beings. Since its design includes the potential for much more pain and suffering, we must not avoid asking why.

We cannot be considered fit creatures, even if we live to be over a hundred. Cockroaches are more fit. They will survive atomic war. We are much more susceptible to disease and slower to heal than animals. Human skin is tight-fitting, and wounds are thus open to infection and need suturing. Animal skin is loose and heals more easily. Since our lives are prolonged, we will suffer more of the negative effects of aging than animals, which tend to die before they become aged and infirm. About 50 percent of all gorillas never reach the age of six. They do not even have a chance to feel the effects of arthritis. Occasionally, an elephant whose eyes have been blinded by a hunter will survive in the wild. But not often. Death is nature's protection in the animal world. Long life often seems to be a characteristically human cause.

The body human itself may give clues as to the purpose of our pain and suffering. The body is sensitive to pain by design. Pain tells me something I need to know. When something in the environment is dangerous, my body alerts me with pain. Since I do not pay much attention to the small irritants, my body has the ability to turn up the volume when the danger is exceptionally great. The person who feels no pain—the leper or the quadriplegic—is exposed and defenseless to environmental dangers, and the body pays the price.

But why does the signal have to be painful? What I need is information from my body, a clicking noise that says my hand is touching a hot stove, or a flashing red light that says I have been sitting in one position too long. The answer is obvious. It would take too long to translate the meaning of the information I would receive in that way. There would be endless streams of clicking noises and flashing lights. One reason for pain is that by the time I understood a different type of message, even if in a second's time, my hand would be burned. Pain, however, is instantly deciphered and immediately clear as to the urgency of the task, although even pain has problems getting through when our minds are occupied elsewhere. The football player keeps running after he sprains an ankle. He scores a touchdown and does not feel the pain until later. A second reason for pain is that we are not designed to receive raw information but to *experience* stimuli. The mind handles experience and awareness. We do not "see" formulae describing contrast ratios or the wavelength content of our visual world. We see our grandmother in her rocking chair. Computers receive information. We see, hear, taste, smell, and feel. Painful experience, while not as desirable as pleasurable experience, has the advantage of creating a more rapid and more motivated response from us. How much pain we experience, however, is in part a function of the mind.

Behind the curtain of life's pain is the specter of inevitable death. The finality of life's end creates a crisis in all thinking minds. Not only is the fear of the unknown or of nonbeing present, but the thought of certain death in the future undermines the values of the present. Imagine that you have just found out that you have terminal cancer and will die within thirty days. What will you do during your last thirty days on earth? Life's activities, aspirations, and even pleasures are suddenly stripped of their meaning. There is an exam tomorrow. Are you going to study? Who cares whether or not you get an *A* on the exam? You will never finish the course. Why should you continue on your diet? Does it really matter if you gain five pounds in the next thirty days? Certain death can rob life of its essence and meaning. The only reason people are able to tolerate it is that they refuse to think about death and push it away as something that occurs in the distant future. But the more we age and agonize through pain and suffering, the more the meaninglessness of life confronts us. Unless there is some other world to which this life is headed, a world from which this life's decisions and values derive meaning, then life is absurd.

What is interesting about the whole drama of pain and suffering and death is that only one species on the planet is concerned by the whole state of affairs. Nature in the wild is a giant cafeteria with each animal eating another, and no animal is "mental" enough to cry "Stop!" Annie Dillard, in her *Pilgrim at Tinker Creek*, describes a bee-eating wasp that has caught a honeybee and is eating honey from its mouth.[4] Suddenly the wasp is grabbed by a praying mantis. The hunter suddenly became prey. As the mantis eats the wasp, the wasp continues to stuff itself with honey. There are some horrible spectacles occurring in nature right under our feet. But in untamed nature there is no outcry of horror. Nature is amoral. Life goes on for the herd when an old zebra is dragged down and eaten by lions. The zebras do not even bother to leave the vicinity of the bloody meal.

It may not concern zebras, but death does concern human beings. We know something is wrong. It bothers us that crimes occur, that animals die in forest fires, that millions of Jews were gassed. It is not right for babies to die, for injustice to reign, for great pain to afflict children. Instead of condemning God for allowing evil in the world, we ought to back up and notice that only one creature is offended by evil. Man stands apart from the animal world and asks "Why?" Where is there meaning in all of this life of pain and toil? Is there any absolute value in life's activities? What is the purpose of these few years we have? The Book of Ecclesiastes makes us think. A beautiful Colorado mountain scene makes us wonder. Steinbeck's *East of*

---

4. Dillard, *Pilgrim at Tinker Creek.*

Eden makes us grieve. Virtually everything turns us into philosophers. When we feel the world deeply through pain and through pleasure, but especially through pain, we are forced to come to grips with the unanswered questions of life. Pain and death are not enjoyable, but they are good teachers, perhaps our most diligent teachers, and they grow more persistent as we age.

A strong awareness of the death of another is possible for higher animals, although we might guess that the presence of death to an animal is only physiologically upsetting or something that is unexpected and frightening. A rhesus monkey may cling to her dead infant for weeks, until it is a mere shred of skin. When an infant chimpanzee's mother dies, the little chimp will sit for long periods alone, rocking from side to side. Jane van Lawick-Goodall tells of a time when some of the chimpanzees she was studying got polio.[5] It is noteworthy that no chimpanzee attempted to help those who were paralyzed. The stricken chimpanzees either died or were shot by the researchers out of compassion. First, the chimpanzees reacted in fear to see a paralyzed chimpanzee dragging itself around by the arms. Then they either reacted with total indifference or attacked the infirm one. There was one exception, a chimpanzee named Humphrey, who would sit near the paralyzed McGregor or wait for him when the rest of the group had moved on. Humphrey came to McGregor's assistance when he was attacked, but Humphrey never groomed him or fed him. Since these two chimpanzees were genetically related and raised in the same family, there may be genetic bonds, which we do not fully understand, that brought Humphrey to McGregor's assistance. The death of McGregor seemed hard on Humphrey, and he kept returning

5. Jane van Lawick-Goodall, *In the Shadow of Man* (Boston: Houghton Mifflin Co., 1971).

for six months to the last place he had seen McGregor. But it is hard to imagine that death meant anything to Humphrey other than the absence of a familiar companion. And the concept of one's own death would be totally foreign to any animal.

To us, death is the cessation of the personality as we know it. The concept of death makes us think and hope. The long life-span we have, the constant presence of pain and suffering, and the vision of one's own death will not let us forget the hardest questions of our hearts. We have been given many years to search out what life offers, to test the meaning we have discovered, to read the sacred Scriptures, to enjoy the innocent pleasures. Not only is there more time to question, but the questions come quite naturally from pained lips and suffering hearts. The questions grow more frequent with age. Animals do not need the time, because they have no questions. But neither could they hear the answers. With us, over time, there is a sufficient answer for living, if we would but hear it.

The body human is designed by God with our ultimate end in mind, and it does its job well until that end. It allows us to feel the world, pain and all, not just to know about it but to experience it fully. It gives us time to perceive the lack of meaning in a world of pain and death. It gives us time to ask the hard questions—and to hear God's answers.

Epilogue:

In the Image of God

Man is the only creature who blushes or needs to.

The body human is a substantial distraction in the orderly, natural theory of human origins. Thus, there no longer seems to be any reason to question our uniqueness among the creatures of planet earth. Our peerless biological features are highly complex, and no prior attenuated versions of them have been substantiated as existing in the animal world. Fossil man, as a supposed connecting link, is of no help to the evolutionist in this regard. Whenever we have had sufficient fossil remains to reconstruct the features of fossil man, we have observed all of the unique ingredients of the human body present in a well-developed form. A recent discovery of the fossil remains of a twelve-year-old male *Homo erectus* showed that the five-foot-six-inch youth would have reached six feet had he lived.[1] This remarkable find specifically counters the assumption that all early humans were smaller than modern man.

To suggest that all the unique human features evolved entirely within the time-span of man's life on earth, however long, demands more than can be provided by adaptive changes within a species. Unexplained by an evolutionary

1. *USA Today,* 19 October 1984, p. 6 D.

record are the human facial muscles, nose, out-turned lips, earlobes, chin, throat, naked skin, sweat-gland system, thermoregulatory capabilities, the female breast, orgasm, and hymen, the long maturation span, the speech center and hemispheric specializations within the brain, the human heel and arch, locking knees, curved spine, re-designed pelvis, buttock muscles, opposable thumbs, an unusually long life-span—and more. For not one of these human features do we find any sufficient connecting links to the animal world.

The fact that so many unique biological differences have occurred in a single "animal," the human being, also directs us to the conclusion that design, not chance, was important in the formation of the human body. All of the unique features of the body human are not merely chance developments for physical survival; they relate to the expression of personhood in human beings. God created persons after *his* image as a person and appropriately gave them "personal" bodies. Personhood is not equivalent to such physiological ingredients as a speech center, opposable thumbs, upright posture, and superior thermoregulatory mechanisms. The accounts of feral children have showed us that even with all the unique biological features present in a human being, personhood does not just "happen." Although personhood's distinguishing features of intelligence, symbolic communication, creativity, moral sensitivity, and emotional depth are potentially present at birth, they must be coaxed forth in a personal environment. Personhood in human beings came about in a universe that was already personal. Personhood could not have spontaneously sprung from an impersonal universe. In a universe without God, we would all be feral children.

The marvelous thing about our existence as persons is

that we resemble the God of the universe, who is a person. We can sense the uniqueness of our personhood when we relate to our animal pets. We interact with them at a level below our own nature, on a physical, vaguely emotional level. We are overbuilt for relating to animals. We were created in the image of God in order to relate to him personally. He created animals, it seems, for our use and our enjoyment. But he created *us*, for a personal relationship with himself and with each other.

The Weight of Personhood

Personhood has not been an easy weight for humans to bear. Consider the animal world. What significant cares or worries can enter the head of a fly or a cow? Of all creatures, only man is capable of becoming mentally ill, because mental illness represents a variety of disturbances in different aspects of personhood, particularly in the intellect, emotions, will, and imagination. The ability to move from knowledge to meaning and to have higher motivations is also involved.

Man is also the only animal who blushes or needs to. He alone blushes with embarrassment and shame, because everything matters to him. When something upsets the order around us, we cry or laugh or blush. Animals are not capable of any of these reactions. When we feel out of order with things around us, we sometimes blush with embarrassment. If you are eating in a fine restaurant and your lobster slips off the plate into your lap, you blush. The autonomic nervous system, responding to the mental stress of what a lobster-in-the-lap means about you, increases blood flow to your body's muscles and skin, particularly to your face. You flush red, and your personhood is on display.

Man is also the only animal who seems outraged at evil, as if it is a distortion in the harmony and meaning of the universe. It bothers us that snakes swallow rabbits whole, that spiders suck flies dry, that a parent repeatedly burns a two-year-old child with a cigarette. To say that we are "horrified" is to use a more appropriate word. Man is the only creature who has a sense of morality. It is interesting that we have a higher sense of morality than we can live up to. This, too, is an expression of our personhood and the image we bear. We legislate against theft, murder, and disorderly conduct. We expect kindness, patience, and love. We may not demand humor or athletic ability or even beauty in our friends, but we do insist on that which is moral—a strange and uniquely personal word. Our own behavior is a constant disappointment to us. Apparently, we are the only creatures who can feel moral guilt and shame at our own immorality and defeats. Since we are also intensely private beings, we avoid exposure of our inner person. Man is the only creature for whom defecation and lovemaking are intensely private happenings. We seem so clearly made for a world other than this one, a world in which there are moral expectations and the capabilities to reach them. When we gaze long at ourselves, the ancient Genesis record rings true. Something went wrong with the original world and our ability to live in it, but not with our desire to live in conformity with who we really are and in the kind of personal world we really inhabit. Something of the original Edenic world has been stamped indelibly on our personhood. It has not been stamped into animals—but exists only in human beings. And though we humans suffer because of the frustrations and shame of living overbuilt for this world, we seem unable to possess the one for which we *were* made.

The Future of Persons

Man is the only creature who shows genius. Geniuses are individuals who cannot be located on the usual continuum of ability or intelligence. They tower above the average member of the species. Animals show no such startling deviations from the norm. Some geniuses seem to be able to analyze the totality of certain sensory experiences and quickly bring the meaningless array into a new synthesis. This form of genius characterized the mind of Albert Einstein, who—at the age of twenty-six—described the theory of relativity.

Other types of geniuses have unusual abilities in a very specific intellectual area such as mathematics. Truman Safford was a Harvard professor at twenty. When asked to square 365,365,365,365,365,365, he took only one minute before replying correctly 133,491,850,208,566,925,016, 658,299,946,583,225.[2] Musical geniuses also seem to appear quite regularly. Mozart, one of the greatest names in music, could, at three, memorize musical passages simply by listening to them once. Before he was seven he was giving piano recitals in the courts of Europe. He wrote minuets at six and his fourteenth symphony when he was only fifteen. Some geniuses mysteriously appear from the ranks of the mentally retarded. Those with the savant syndrome often have a singular, spectacular talent. One such genius is Leslie Lemke, a thirty-two-year-old blind and severely retarded man. At the age of sixteen, Leslie played a Tchaikovsky concerto after having heard it only once. After hearing any piece of music, he can unerringly reproduce it.[3]

2. Gordon R. Taylor, *The Natural History of the Mind* (New York: Penguin Books, 1981) p. 264.

3. *People Magazine*, 2 July 1984, p. 26.

As of yet we do not know why geniuses appear in the human population. Their very existence, though, points out a very important characteristic of the human race. Human beings seem to possess enormous latent abilities. Man gives every appearance of being a creature fallen from some higher state of existence. Hidden abilities, which are occasionally released by biological accidents, give a tantalizing hint of what human life might be designed for. As the Genesis accounts reveal, we were created for more than just a physical existence for a brief three score and ten years. We were designed for an eternity of spiritual, mental, and physical life. After the present life we can experience full humanness, fulfilling every human longing, feeling at home for the first time.

During that eternity we shall not forget our first life on this planet, in this humble human form with its biological limits. These years will have been the prologue to an unending story, the story of God's plan for us. Our bodies have been telling us all along about our personhood and helping to reveal the inherent image of God. The human body is a sign of personhood in this life and of the hope of all that is to come in the next. Such is the glory and the story of the body human.

Bibliography

Asimov, Isaac. *The Human Body: Its Structure and Operation.* Boston: Houghton Mifflin Co., 1963.

———. *The Human Brain: Its Capacities and Functions.* Boston: Houghton Mifflin Co., 1963.

Best, Catherine T., and Harris, Lauren J. "Childhood," in *Annual Editions: Psychology 81/82.* Guilford, CT: The Dushkin Publishing Group, Inc., 1980, pp. 126–129.

Best, C. H., and Taylor, N. B. *The Human Body,* 4th ed. New York: Holt Rinehart and Winston, 1963.

Brandt, Paul, and Yancey, Philip. *Fearfully and Wonderfully Made.* Grand Rapids: Zondervan Publishing House, 1980.

Bronowski, Jacob. *The Ascent of Man.* Boston: Little Brown and Co., 1973.

Carlson, Neil R. *Physiology of Behavior,* 2nd ed. Boston: Allyn and Bacon, Inc., 1980.

Chalmers, Neil. *Social Behavior in Primates.* Baltimore: University Park Press, 1980.

Comfort, Alex. *Ageing: The Biology of Senescence* (rev. ed.). New York: Holt Rinehart and Winston, Inc., 1964.

Cosgrove, Mark. *The Essence of Human Nature.* Grand Rapids: Zondervan Publishing House, 1977.

———. *Psychology Gone Awry.* Grand Rapids: Zondervan Publishing House, 1979.

Custance, Arthur. *Evolution or Creation?* Grand Rapids: Zondervan Publishing House, 1976.

Darwin, Charles. *The Expression of Emotions in Man and Animals*. Chicago: The University of Chicago Press, 1965.

Dixson, A. F. *The Natural History of the Gorilla*. London: Weidenfeld and Nicolson, 1981.

Dubos, Rene. *So Human an Animal*. New York: Charles Scribner's, 1968.

Eckstein, Gustav. *The Body Has a Head*. New York: Harper and Row, 1969.

Eimerl, Sarel, and DeVore, Irven. *The Primates*. New York: Time-Life Books, 1965.

Ellis, Havelock. *Psychology of Sex*. New York: The New American Library, 1933.

Feldman, Philip, and MacCulloch, Malcolm. *Human Sexual Behavior*. New York: John Wiley and Sons, 1980.

Finch, Caleb, and Hayflick, Leonard, eds. *Handbook of the Biology of Aging*. New York: Van Nostrand Reinhold Co., 1977.

Foelix, Rainer. *Biology of Spiders*. Cambridge, Mass.: Harvard University Press, 1982.

Fossey, Dian. "The Imperiled Mountain Gorilla," *National Geographic*, April 1981, pp. 500–523.

Gersh, Eileen, and Gersh, Isidore. *Biology of Women*. Baltimore: University Park Press, 1981.

Groves, Philip, and Schlesinger, Kurt. *Biological Psychology*, 2nd ed. Dubuque, IA: Wm. C. Brown Co. Publishers, 1979.

Hardy, Richard. *Temperature and Animal Life*, 2nd ed. Baltimore: University Park Press, 1979.

Klots, Alexander, and Klots, Elsie. *1001 Questions Answered About Insects*. New York: Dodd, Mead and Co., 1961.

Lamb, Marion. *Biology of Ageing*. New York: John Wiley and Sons, 1977.

Langley, Lee, and Christensen, John. *Structure and Function of the Human Body: An Introduction to Anatomy and Physiology*. Minneapolis: Burgess Publishing Co., 1978.

LeGross-Clark, W. E. *The Antecedents of Man*, 3rd ed. Chicago: Quadrangle Books, 1971.

Mitchell, G. *Human Sex Differences: A Primatologist's Perspective*. New York: VanNostrand Reinhold Co., 1981.

Morris, Desmond. *The Naked Ape*. New York: Dell Publishing Co., Inc., 1969.

Pines, Maya. "The Human Difference," *Psychology Today,* September 1983, pp. 62–68.

Podolsky, Doug, and the Editors of US News Books. *Skin: The Human Fabric.* Washington, D.C.: US News Books, 1982.

Rajecki, D. W. *Comparing Behavior: Studying Man, Studying Animals.* Hillsdale, NJ: Lawrence Erlbaum Associates, Publishers, 1983.

Restak, Richard. "The Origins of Violence," *Saturday Review,* May 12, 1979, pp. 16–19.

Reynolds, Vernon. *The Biology of Human Action,* 2nd ed. San Francisco: W. H. Freeman, 1980.

Robinson, Daniel, and Uttal, William. *Foundations of Psychobiology.* New York: Macmillan Publishing Co., 1983.

Rosenweig, Mark, and Leiman, Arnold. *Physiological Psychology.* Lexington, Mass.: D.C. Heath and Co., 1982.

Sagan, Carl. *The Dragons of Eden.* New York: Ballantine Books, 1977.

Shock, Nathan, ed. *Biological Aspects of Aging.* New York: Columbia University Press, 1962.

Singh, J.A.L., and Zingg, Robert. *Wolf-children and Feral Man.* New York: Harper and Brothers Publishers, 1939.

Slijper, Everhard. *Whales and Dolphins.* Ann Arbor: The University of Michigan Press, 1976.

Springer, Sally, and Deutsch, Georg. *Left Brain Right Brain.* San Francisco: W. H. Freeman and Co., 1981.

Strehler, Bernard, ed. *The Biology of Aging.* Washington DC: American Institute of Biological Sciences, 1960.

Swanson, Carl. *The Natural History of Man.* Englewood Cliffs, NJ: Prentice Hall, 1973.

Swindler, Davis, and Wood, Charles. *An Atlas of Primate Gross Anatomy: Baboon, Chimpanzee, and Man.* Seattle: University of Washington Press, 1973.

Tanner, James, and Taylor, Gordon. *Growth.* New York: Time, Inc., 1965.

Taylor, Gordon. *The Natural History of the Mind.* New York: Penguin Books, 1981.

Tuttle, Russell, ed. *Primate Functional Morphology and Evolution.* Paris: Mouton Publishers, 1975.

van Lawick-Goodall, Jane. *In the Shadow of Man.* Boston: Houghton Mifflin Co., 1971.

Vincent, Clard, ed. *Human Sexuality in Medical Education and Practice.* Springfield, IL: Charles C. Thomas Publisher, 1968.

Wilson, Clifford. *The Language Gap.* Grand Rapids, MI: Zondervan Publishing House, 1984.